Scribe Publications
OUR FATHER WHO WASN'T THERE

David Carlin teaches media production and writing at RMIT University, Melbourne. He is the author of plays, including *Frankenstein's Children*, and the writer and director of short films and documentaries, including *Out of Our Minds*. His work has been performed and screened in Australia and internationally. He has also directed numerous new Australian plays, as well as Circus Oz. This is his first book of creative non-fiction.

OUR FATHER WHO WASN'T THERE
DAVID CARLIN

SCRIBE
Melbourne

Scribe Publications Pty Ltd
PO Box 523
Carlton North, Victoria, Australia 3054
Email: info@scribepub.com.au

First published by Scribe 2010
Copyright © David Carlin 2010

Typeset in 12/19 pt Adobe Caslon Pro by the publishers. Printed and bound in Australia by Griffin Press. Only wood grown from sustainable regrowth forests is used in the manufacture of paper found in this book.

National Library of Australia
Cataloguing-in-Publication data

Carlin, David.

Our Father Who Wasn't There

9781921640254 (pbk.)

1. Carlin, Brian.   2. Carlin, David.   3. Fathers and sons — Western Australia — Biography.   4. Father and infant — Western Australia — Biography.   5. Loss (Psychology).

306.874209941

This project has been assisted by
the Australian Government through
the Australia Council for the Arts,
its arts funding and advisory body.

Quote at p. 200 from Ronald Kessler, *The Sins of the Father: Joseph P. Kennedy and the dynasty he founded*, Grand Central Publishing

www.scribepublications.com.au

To Linda

A Partial Sketch of Family Connections

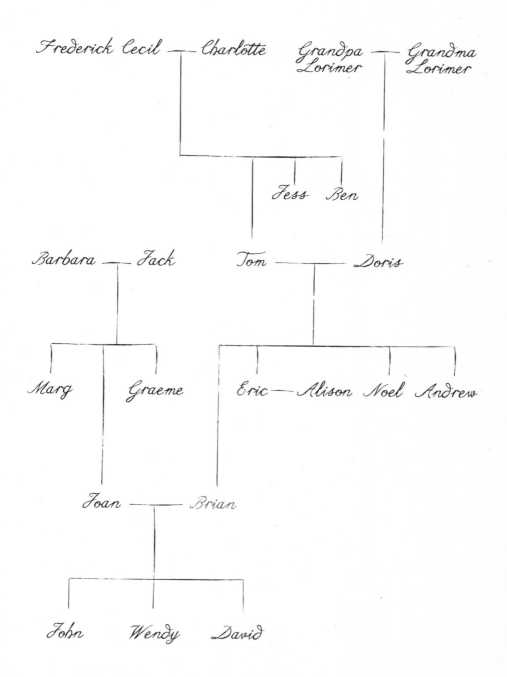

Chapter One

I am here but I am not here. I am a baby, six months old, lying in a cot, helpless, arms waving, fingers gripping and ungripping, catching at the world so large and noisy around me.

It is January 1964, just a few months after JFK was killed in faraway America, a time of violence and high passion, Marilyn fading, screaming mop-hair on the rise. Clean-cut boys are hunting communists in the jungle. Even at this end of the wireless, in this quiet country town under the flag of Menzies, the knives are out — at least in my father's mind.

There is a man and a woman and two children and a baby in a weatherboard house on a suburban street in a town too small for suburbs. Bridgetown, Western Australia.

I am there and I am not there. An eye-witness without an 'I'. A baby sucking in evidence, absorbing hungrily, aware but uncomprehending. I am the baby but I can never reach the baby. No matter how far back I travel, looting my memory for the faintest snatch — a moment in the bushes with a cousin, the sailing ship at the end of the blankets — I can't get near. The baby is away, away, down the end of a long corridor, behind heavy doors, locked. It exists only because it had to exist, logically.

My father must have looked at that baby. He must have spoken to that baby. Perhaps, in the quiet of night, he told the baby secrets. He let it wrap its tiny fingers around one of his huge ones, and they wrestled. When it bawled, he even picked up the baby, stretched like a kitten and then folded awkwardly into the crook of an arm across his chest.

When he died, the baby was six months and nine days old. Did he let it into his confidence? Did he know what he would do that fine hot day?

By my mother's bed — which, in my memory, was wider than a single but smaller than a double, and thus showed that she was neither a child nor intending to be sharing it with anyone other than me on a Sunday morning, listening to the eight o'clock radio drama for children — on her bedside table, was a black-and-white photo of my father standing outside a house. Viewed slightly from below, he was looking off into the middle distance. Any hint of the heroic was undercut by a softness in his cheeks, by his clothes: woollen vest over long-sleeved shirt.

This photo, never referred to, stood as a sign of her continuing allegiance. She wasn't hiding him away. And neither was she hiding anything from him. This small photograph, propped up in its cheap tin-and-glass frame, was the only trace of him in the house. (Had the small collection of tools in the garage been his, or did they come from my pop, Jack, my mother's father?) There were no family photo albums, no other pictures of him on the walls, no bag of golf clubs in the cupboard or old school trophy in a glass cabinet. Just this photo on the bedside table. Not on the mantelpiece in the lounge room, where it might have been up for grabs in any number of semi-public situations: the rellies' bunfight on a Sunday evening, so-and-so dropping in for a cup of tea, a stray friend drifted in from the street. The bedside table, a private space, peaceful as a library. Close to her heart, her dreamself.

I knew who it was in the photo, although I don't know how. She must have told me, I suppose, back when I asked questions. (She told me: 'One day he went to sleep and never woke up.')

The photo was a map of a faraway country. There is the idea of China, and now here is the shape of China; and the shape helps to put a boundary around the idea because, whatever China is or may turn out to be, it will forever fit within that beautifully intricate and specific shape. So 'Dad', or 'my father', or even 'Brian' had a definite shape, and there it was, on the bedside table.

There he was, constant and defined but like an old film-set, a two-dimensional image leaning in thin air, hiding as much as it revealed.

❧

My mother cries every time she talks about him. Which is rarely, and only if I bring it up. I haven't told her yet that I am writing this. I will tell her soon.

Has anyone actually died from having a story told? Died of shock, of grief, of having everything long-forgotten gushed up to the surface and strewn across the landscape? Of sheer heartache?

The cognitive therapist, Mr B., tells me it can only be a good thing: flush it out and everyone feels better. But how can he be so sure? He seems to picture a cleansing ritual, Korean-bathhouse style, where I imagine a ghastly, vulgar exhibition, like those contemporary art shows featuring internal organs. Maybe I'll feel better and they'll feel worse, which will spoil me feeling better, so I'll feel worse, and we'll all feel worse, and my mother might quite possibly die.

I went through this scenario with Mr B., who scoffed. Scoffing is a bedside manner he likes to employ in these situations.

She will be supportive. She will think it's her fault. But why do I want to drag them through it? Am I punishing them for just getting along with life?

It all seems absurd, as Mr B. asserts, when you look at it from a safe distance. But, from the inside, the pressure is immense and powerful.

What right do I have to tell this story?

∾

One of the first things I knew about my father was that he refused to eat lettuce. I may have been 12 when Barbara, my maternal grandmother, told me this. His stance, she reported, was on the grounds that lettuce was 98 per cent water, and therefore a waste of time.

By this time, approaching 90, Barbara took the stairs slowly, despite still walking every morning into the icy Southern Ocean. (Her secret to vitality: don't wash the salt off until evening.) I remember her sitting in her wool-clad green recliner by the window over Albany's Middleton Beach, with her single late-afternoon sherry, a fond smile softening her cracking, powdered face. She liked him, in spite of everything. He made her laugh. 'He was a good man, Brian.'

Not a bad man, in spite of everything. In spite of how one might feel about him.

The water in the bay at Middleton is sheltered by the lee of a granite headland. The sea is cold and calm. At an early seven o'clock, the prospect is deliciously unbearable, sliding into frozen vodka.

I descend, inch by inch, muscles tensed, disciplining the shock of the water into a slow, inexorable rise up my skinny legs as they push out towards the two islands, Michaelmas and Breaksea. Like the thick fluid-rise in a thermometer, if up meant colder. A front line is briefly drawn across the upper thigh, before the plunge to navel necessary to get past the balls as quickly as possible, and then the further dip to chest. Breathe and soak up all protest. Look around. The sunken summer trampolines lie still behind their fences on the buffalo grass above the beach. The sea, a grey restorative fluid within the curve of the bay, is sparsely dotted with the bathing caps of the elderly exercise set.

I hurl myself out and under, tossing out arms and legs in a

freestyle faster than the cold. When I stroll casually from the water, knees against seaweed, the elements are vanquished. I notice orange sunlight in the pine trees, seagulls cutting the sky, a car winding down the long hill around the headland from Albany. There is no better feeling than early-morning salt on cold flesh and the prospect of hot breakfast. This is the reward for Protestant self-mastery, Scottish grit.

⁊

As for Brian: he'd let himself go. He'd flopped and dropped, and somehow lost his way in endless ticktock running around and ruminations in his scone, open the floodgates and all hell comes loose, yabber yabber cacophony, broken record broken record broken record. I should, he shouldn't; I should, you should; I can't, I should; I can't, I should; gallop gallop, gallop gallop. Racing off into the never-never. Don Quixote tilting. Excessive in the head.

Unlike Tom, his father. The arch-villain of the piece, the Tom-cat, spraying all and sundry with his poison. If I'm making him out fit for melodrama, he'd be in the flesh altogether too dull and drear, upright clipped, and backbone stony to play himself. You'd need a middle-aged Olivier or an Anthony Hopkins, good at doing thin mouth, tension in the cheeks, and way-back bitterness turned hard.

Let him just make an entrance, even if I imagine it: clodding across the muddy oval at Perth Modern School in full military attire in 1941, towards a soggy line of boys. He will allow the rain to drip off his nose as he stands before them, and thus demonstrate full military willpower. He will bark commands at them, and thus show what is expected of cadets in any weather, what boys must do to call themselves men. He's the genuine article, an army sergeant-major, generously volunteering his time to the school once a week, on a Thursday, to lead the cadet corps in this time of war, with a son, B. F. Carlin, in Form Two (currently, third from the right, shoulders slightly drooping, socks cold and wet).

'Carlin!'

'Yes, sir.'

'Stand up straight, son! Show me your chest, son!' Shouting against the westerly. Pushing back the wind. No special treatment. None perceived, none given.

Tom's nickname, whispered, preceded him across the oval. 'Bull', that's what they called him in the army. Bull Carlin.

But more about him later.

∽

The silence in our lives growing up was a demure, suburban, well-creased-bedspread type of silence. If we had been missing, say, a dining-room table but, say again, some of our neighbours had one, while others ate at ultra-modern breakfast bars or in the kitchen or even on their knees in front of the black-and-white TV, well, then, that would not be too odd. But missing a father was something that stood out, especially in that day and age, because back then everybody seemed to have one.

'Don't you have a father?' kids would ask at school.

No.'

'Why not?'

'He died.'

This powerful and dramatic statement was usually enough to shut them up, but if they did come back with 'How?' the answer was: 'Because of the war.' This answer was large enough in all its shadowy mystery to forestall further discussion.

We were a close family, mother, my two siblings John and Wendy, and I, who might have been called Michael to complete the Peter Pan family had not my cousin taken the name a year earlier. We never argued. Of course there were squabbles between the children, but nothing serious. Ruptures were rare enough to be horrifying, like the time when I was five or six and provoked my mother to the point of her opening the kitchen drawer and gripping the wooden spoon. Suddenly, I was aware of how far I'd pushed her, and was filled with shame and remorse. She didn't even raise the wooden spoon in my direction, but I could see the pain she was in, and knew I had to protect her.

We were survivors and needed to band together, bearing our unspeakable loss. This I knew, although not consciously. My mother's immense strength and practical, capable nature belied a fragility that we must not puncture. Inside her, as in a picture-book melodrama, were rivers of pain that could burst forth and drown us all. Inside her was the apocalypse, storms that would rip off sheets of corrugated iron, tremors that would tear away all solid earth and open the abyss. If we were careful to stay on high ground, where the grass was clipped and neat and the sun smiled, we would be okay. We would survive.

INSIDE HIM was the apocalypse. Nobody could understand it. Brian, too, had his high ground. He was the charming, dapper man-about-town. He was suave and well loved. He was sharp and witty. He had a brilliant career. He had everything going for him.

℘

There are files. No cross-sections of brain preserved in aspic (for obvious reasons). Files. Handwritten notes later transcribed on typewriter by a horn-rimmed secretary whacking into carbon. Doctors' notes, test results, official correspondence. These files I discovered in early 1995 at the Australian Archives branch in Perth's Victoria Park, across the Swan River from where I was staying with my aunt Alison and uncle Eric, closest in age to Brian of his three brothers.

Brian was 'in the war'. This, at least, was always known: he had been 'in the war'. And what he'd died of — it was *something to do with the war.* Some shrapnel in the leg, the Japs deep in the jungle, gone gangrenous many years later, there was nothing anyone could do, eating him away gradually from the inside … am I getting close?

When I was 11, I loved to read those small-format Combat comic books; we used to sneak them into school. The Second World War was the real war, the capitalised War, in which we were the good guys and the Germans and Japs were so obviously the bad guys; just the way they dressed, to begin with, and their insignia, their nasty colours, black and red … and *yellow* … We were Captain Mainwaring and the Dambusters, and they were Colonel Klink and kamikaze finger-torturers and Hitler; and we were Churchill on the beach and English and American, and they spoke in those strange, guttural, harsh languages, and were dark … and *yellow* … This was not like Vietnam, which we watched on television, to where your older brother might be sent to fight if his birthday came up on the screen; and where nobody ever won anything, it just went on and on with people dying and no one even sure who to barrack for.

Alison suggested that we could probably find Brian's medical records. She found a phone number for me. My father's nervous condition had been attributed to his war service, therefore he had received treatment under the Veterans' Affairs Repatriation system, records of which were kept by the department in case-files and deposited with the Australian Archives in Victoria Park.

I drove out there with my wife, Linda, one fine day in our hire car. We found a low, flat-roofed red-brick building on a plain suburban street. It resembled an over-sized school library that would have been the departmental pride circa 1975. The place was deserted.

I filled in an application to view the personal records of Brian F. Carlin. We were let into the search room with our visitor's badges, numbered 01 and 02.

After a short wait, an official named Tony arrived with the files. His voice was professionally neutral: 'What do you know about your father?'

This was a test. But I knew what he wanted to hear: 'My

father committed suicide, having suffered, over a long period of time, a mental illness associated in some way with his war service.'

Tony seemed satisfied. He told me that my father's records had never been viewed, and that, in granting me access, I should understand that they would henceforth be open for anyone to see. Such is the power of the archive-keeper. Here he was, with row upon row of private lives and private deaths neatly stacked in alphabetical order. Each one a chronology of secrets, an elliptical narrative of symptoms and treatments, hastily scribbled medical notes, official forms, and letters. Each one a war story, the traces left by the processing of a human being through a particular system of rules, regulations, and knowledges. They were stories of what went wrong, over time, and what was done about it, or not done, each following the unique arc of a particular trauma — some, presumably, starting dramatically, with a horrific injury in battle, and continuing in a straightforward fashion.

But how many more were like my father's, an accretion of details in the face of gaps, absences, and mysteries?

Tony returned with three files, each between one- and three-inches thick, their worn, brown covers torn and fraying, with crisp, white folders over the top labelled: 'not to be opened unless access approved'. These he plumped on the desk in front of us, before retreating once more into the depths of the building.

I opened the files. Inside were sheets of paper, mostly handwritten, some typed: psychiatrists' reports; daily hospital records; notes from one doctor to another, regarding his condition or discussing treatment; letters from his workplace, from the life-insurance company; from himself, requesting an appointment with a specialist. At the end were copies of official police documents.

IN HER DEPOSITION to the police, *Mrs Carlin* (my mother) said that Brian had gone out that day appearing normal and cheerful, and giving no indication that he was contemplating taking his own life.

His work as an extension officer for the Western Australian Department of Agriculture had him often on the road, visiting farms in the district. That day, he was due to stay out overnight, to return late the following afternoon. It was late January, when the grass was brown and the creeks dry. The little village of Bridgetown was shuttered down against the heat of an east wind. Dogs stretched themselves along any patch of cool, shady ground that they could find.

My mother had a lot to do, with two small children to amuse in their school holidays and a six-month-old baby to attend to. But, in the quiet of the evening, with the house thrown open at last to catch any whiff of cool breeze, she must have wondered, yet again, whether this would be the time.

He'd tried suicide before: three times in as many years. Once, he'd cut his wrists, and he'd twice taken overdoses of medications, the last time wandering in the sand dunes by Burns Beach. He'd been better lately, out of hospital and back at work for several months, but any time he was away she worried for him.

The next evening he didn't appear, and she spent a sleepless night listening for the sound of the car turning into the driveway. She must have slept briefly before dawn, because the baby woke her with a jolt. She stuck him on her breast and fought against the fear rising in her. There could be any number of explanations for her husband's absence. He might well ring soon and explain how the car broke down late, and how he wasn't near a phone so couldn't call, how he'd slept in it overnight and this morning found friendly farmers to help get him going. He'd be home by lunchtime; perhaps they could have something to eat together before he went back to the office?

She waited. The kids woke up and came in wanting breakfast. Wendy said, 'Where's Dad?'

My mother fought back the urge to burst into tears. 'He's still out working.'

Leaving the baby asleep in his cot, she bustled out into the kitchen to commence the rituals of the day. She should call Stan Hardisty, Brian's boss at the local Agriculture Department office. She should let him know, she should ask for help in finding Brian. But maybe Brian would still ring. She could still hope, whereas once she called Stan her fears might be confirmed.

It wasn't until two o'clock in the afternoon, with the kids next door with the neighbours, that she picked up the phone and called Stan. Stan assumed that Brian had been at home. He tried to be reassuring, promising that he'd find out what had happened and get back to her. She, for her part, was quiet.

౿౩

I've told her now. I sent her an email — no, she sent me an email, casually asking me what I was working on. So I had to tell her.

After a few days of worrying, I wrote it down quickly one morning. Clear, honest, but not too emotionally demanding: grown-up. This was the tone I went for. Linda thought it was fine. I sent it off, and we went away on holiday for four days.

The day after we got back, she rang but only spoke to my daughter, Esther, as I had an interstate visitor and she didn't want to interrupt. I rang back. She wasn't there. I left a message. She rang back. I wasn't there. She left a message. She went away for four days on her own holiday.

The night after she got back, she called. I leapt into conversation: 'How was your holiday? ... Oh, where is that national park? ... Is it nice? ... How far is it from Adelaide? ... And did you have a nice time when all the grandchildren were over? ... No, I haven't spoken to you since then ... How was Kangaroo Island? ... How was Jonny? ... Did he have a good time? ... Did everyone get on well together? ... Did you get my email? ... And what did you think?'

Fine. She thinks it's fine.

'And you don't mind me — ?'

'No, of course not.'

'Oh, good! Yes, study's going well, it's all going well, very busy, never seem to have enough time; but it's going well, yes.'

'Wendy left a message for me, I must ring her. Did you hear about the house in France? The roof collapsed!'

'No! Really? No, I haven't spoken to Wendy for a little while, what happened? What will they do?'

On we go with the dance of conversation. And it's good and it's fine, and we've spoken about it and she knows about it, and she doesn't want to talk about it, and that's fine. It's all fine. She didn't cry. She didn't get upset. We skipped across it lightly, as if we were talking about borrowing a recipe book.

Chapter Two

As soon as he finished high school, Brian joined the navy. He had just turned seventeen. As my uncle Eric told me later in a letter:

> He had always wanted to be in the navy. He was a great reader. He read all the *Just William* books, then on to Jeffery Farnol and another writer, Humphrey someone, who both wrote endless sea stories. He had an undimmed view of the naval life ...

Brian came across from Perth to Melbourne on the train in early 1945 for training at the HMAS *Cerberus* naval base at Crib Point on the Mornington Peninsula.

Crossing the vastness of the Nullarbor, he found himself,

as does every Western Australian venturing out for the first time, passing through the end of the world, crawling up the monumental wall of pure horizons to catch a glimpse of what lies beyond.

Leaving Perth and winding through the Darling Escarpment, out across the wheat belt and past the goldfields of Kalgoorlie, time is sucked backwards. Behind the coastal veneer of modernity one finds convict-built colonial outposts and tin-flapping golden ghost towns. As settled civilisation drains away and the last paddock squares dissolve into the saltpans, the country itself quietens. Hills become contours become indentations become the sheer-planed earth itself. Trees twist and stunt and duck until they are merely bushes. Bushes that had seemed low shrivel to neat balls, far from the sky. The land is quiet and hollow, limestone-eggshell hollow, with the lapping waters of ancient seas beneath. The train no longer twists and turns but, paying attention to the place, stills itself and heads due east.

This is a country of fine detail and patience. Whatever is unnecessary and excessive has been removed, all sign of origin and destination. For hour upon hour, the land beneath the train kicks away, its speed slowing with geometrical precision the further from the window it goes until, at the mocking horizon, there is no movement at all.

Childhood ended for Brian here in the Nullarbor. His mother and father vanished behind him in the west, together with the life they had created for him. Henceforth, he would make his own way.

Out of this blue, clean daylight mist, sooner or later would emerge the answer: a smudge of red dirt clumping outlandishly a few feet high, a distant mark on the horizon, an irregularity, a badly drawn grey-black line that might signify where the other world begins. That will be the real world, or at least its beginning — the world known from books and newspapers and newsreels, so much better drawn than the sandy shadow-shacks of home.

Finally, I imagine there is a station, a solid stump of a building propped up by a few trees. The train has almost forgotten how to stop, jolting and squealing wearily as it pulls up, awkward with being so long and the station so short.

A man stands in the door, shaded from the sun, watching the train to see how it might be different from all the other ones that have come past this way.

By now, the train corridors are full of people gawking, waving, spitting onto the dirt. There's Brian; I see him pressed against the open window, sticking his head out with the rest of them. A couple of kids in shorts skid around in the red dust, excited by another captive audience. Their dog, a mad kelpie, barks and spins in circles.

The driver jumps down, cigarette in hand, and a guard brings a bag of mail to the stationmaster. The three of them have a quiet chat and a laugh under the tiny verandah while, up and down the corridors, the rest of the train's population strain against their confinement. The doors are locked. This, apparently, is not a scheduled stop for passengers.

Around Brian the crowd is quiet — perhaps novices like him, uncertain of procedures. Western Australians in foreign territory. But, from down the way, in the next carriage, some kind of ruckus is starting, a few heads sticking out the window, calling and singing.

'Jeez, so this is Adelaide!' says one. 'Hey, mate,' now calling to the stationmaster, 'Are we in Adelaide?'

His chorus of supporting heads guffaw. A couple of young women near Brian glance at each other.

'You can almost smell the alcohol from here,' says one. They try not to smile.

'Hey, mate,' calls the wit, still convinced he can get more out of his material: 'I heard it was quiet in Adelaide, but jeez!' Now the chorus chime in. 'Yeah, jeez, where is everybody here in Adelaide?'

Now the front guy has a new line: 'Wait on, I thought it was Darwin the Japs bombed? Musta been Adelaide! Jeez, they did a good job!'

The driver and the stationmaster look over at the youths, but don't stop their conversation. As if they have a few boisterous monkeys secure in a cage.

'Hey, mate, you gonna let us out or what?' calls the head monkey. The driver just chews on his cigarette and grimaces, but the stationmaster holds up the palm of his hand and shakes his head, as if dismissing a commonly held misconception, while continuing his own story to the driver. The guard is ferreting in the mailbag to double-check he's delivering the right items.

An older woman appears in the station doorway with a tray of fresh lemon-cordial for the workingmen.

'Yes, please,' calls out the monkey.

The driver flicks away his fag and takes a glass. He and the guard thank the stationmaster's wife with all due courtesy, and the three men stand and enjoy their refreshment as she melts back into the station. The entire train salivates.

It's the last straw for the chief monkey, who eases himself out backwards onto the windowsill and leaps off into the dirt to the cheers of his troop. Extravagantly, he stretches himself, unshaven and untucked, then turns away and pisses exuberantly. The gang back on the train whoop some more at this display of brazen smartarsery.

The three on the platform don't want to give him too much attention. The driver is lighting up again and spitting out stray tobacco, doing his best to look unimpressed. The kids, though, have given up chucking rocks along the fence line. They want to know what this unpredictable stranger is going to do next. He's definitely brought a fresh new act to this neck of the woods.

'Anybody want to get off?' he yells to the long row of heads facing him along the train. Predictably, his friends roar in the affirmative. But he's looking to broaden his appeal now. 'Anybody want to get off?' he repeats, this time addressing himself further along the train.

'Yes, I do,' says the voice of a middle-aged woman just a few feet back from Brian. As the rest of the carriage turns to examine her, hot and bothered in her tailored mauve suit, she explains, for their benefit, 'I wouldn't mind stretching my legs after being stuck in here all day and night.' No one demurs.

The head monkey grins, hoists up his belt, and tucks in his shirt, so as to come over all gentlemanly. Mimicking the stationmaster, he holds up his hand and shakes his head to his own tribe, and strides down towards his damsel in distress, just one small stumble along the way to further support the drunk hypothesis of the young woman near Brian.

Behind the monkey, the officials mutter among themselves but, in their wisdom or lethargy, make no move to arrest him. Reaching the carriage door, he has difficulty with the latch but enough native wit to turn even this to comic advantage with the crowd. Finally, he stumbles upon the knack of the device, and the door swings open. He proffers a hand to help the mauve-suited woman negotiate the steps to the ground. She promptly casts herself adrift from him and picks her way across the pebbly red dirt in no particular direction, ignoring the applause he's conjured with his arm outstretched theatrically towards her.

Others tumble off the train in her wake, and Brian feels himself swept up in the flow of the undammed river of people pouring out the doorway. Within a moment, he is splashed out to join the others below.

The monkey, since recast as a swashbuckling Fool, is winding his way along the train, opening door after door and, in the other direction, others follow suit. New cascades of passengers emerge in their wake, until the entire length of the train is shadowed by the mass of its inhabitants milling to its side.

No one ventures very far from the security of the nearest door which, after all, represents their lifeline to civilisation. Presumably, they don't want to end up stuck in this godforsaken place; or perhaps they are worried that they won't be able to resist the pull of its uncanny attraction, this teetering outpost on the edge of the deep limestone sea. Surely one or two are fantasising a post as teacher, nurse, even missionary to the Aborigines who must be out there somewhere (although where can they hide in this landscape?).

Others imagine usurping the stationmaster's position, or that of his wife, which may involve smuggling oneself off the train and awaiting one's chance for murder and then seduction. Who would do such a thing? A lonelyheart, a desperado on the run, someone with a penchant for uniforms and patience for the endless wait? Brian reads faces for telltale signs.

The three officials have accepted the unscheduled mass disembarkation without batting a collective eyelid. It seems to Brian that, for them, this is an Act of God, a version of which might happen every day, and which no amount of timetabling or regulation can circumvent. Their phlegmatic demeanour suggests they may have seen far worse. Dancing on the train roof? Fornication in the dust? The virginal boy blushes as if he had just announced his wandering thoughts to the surrounding ladies.

The train driver takes a last suck of his cigarette. If people want to get off the train, what can you do? They'll get back on soon enough when they hear the whistle. He takes his leave of the stationmaster and makes a beeline for the locomotive.

Sure enough, the whistle sounds and the crowds clamber back up.

'All aboard, please, ladies and gentlemen' shouts the guard. 'This train will be departing in two minutes. All aboard that's going aboard!' He makes his way down the line, in case any stragglers have missed his message, and other guards appear to help him secure the doors.

Brian makes his way back to his seat by the window, and allows his eyes to close as the motion of the train picks up again. He remembers the smell of alcohol on his father's breath. Tom coming home in the winter dark to find the four boys laughing with their mother in the kitchen. The light behind him in the doorway. The hush that settled on them, and her now hurrying to tip dinner onto the plates, the boys washing their hands at the laundry trough, a swirl of activity around the still, cold figure checking his watch. A minute before seven: Tom switching on the big wireless in the dining room, taking care to time perfectly the coincidence of the napkin spread on his lap, the wireless warming up to full volume, the anthem for the ABC news and, unless his wife has let him down, some familiar variation of hot meat and three veg. Silence unfurled across the dinner table, the better to concentrate on the plummy baritone of the broadcast.

Back home in Perth, now only three boys join their parents around that table. Brian has been absent for two meals already. He misses the smell of his mother's food, but not his father's breath.

❧

Uncertainty grips me again as I contemplate the wanderings of my story. Here I am with an unscheduled stop in the middle of the desert. My Brian, carrying only his few light pieces of biographical detail, gleaned from anecdote and archive, has found himself surrounded by a throng of passing bit-characters.

Is he planning to make his way in such manner across the

continent to Melbourne, with similar scenes played out in the dining car, his sitting compartment, the station platform in Adelaide? Is he already in uniform, having signed up in Perth, or does he travel in civilian clothes until the commencement of his training over east?

This will surely have great bearing on the way others relate to him. If he's in uniform, they'll talk to him, ask him where he's going, and he'll feel the respect that they accord him, gain confidence in the story he relates — which, unlike mine, as I sometimes feel, is a perfectly respectable one: a youth straight from school who has enlisted to fight for his country in wartime.

Bravely, he ventures across the country to do his duty and cheerfully face whatever perils may await. There is neither more nor less that he has to say. He is only a simple spear-carrier, an extra, one of thousands, but admirable in his naivety, adorably cute and fresh-faced in his costume, and vulnerable enough to tug the heartstrings of the older lady passengers.

He'll find, this uniformed Brian, that the course of the journey announces, in a way that is both pleasurable and unsettling, a whole new version of himself, the independent young man on the cusp of life, the loyal recruit to His Majesty's forces.

As the train stops in the desert, and at other times, people may turn to him as a figure of some authority. If those larrikins threaten to drag proceedings towards a dangerous violence, he may be expected, along with the other men in uniform almost certainly dotted like him through the train, to assert some order. This, the idea of having to physically confront the offenders, is a frankly terrifying prospect that brings him face to face with the vision of his father shaking him by his collar … the disgust in his eyes.

On the train, the ladies around Brian have no idea that their young matinee idol is a coward and a bed-wetter. The uniform is a brittle masquerade; beneath its creases, insignia, and polish, his flesh is soft and weak. He sees himself reflected in his father's eyes: a puppy, not a man.

On the other hand, the Brian not yet uniformed travels incognito, an intriguing stranger; quiet, absorbed in his books. He's perfectly polite but unforthcoming, shy most likely, attracting as little attention as possible. For some, he's almost a ghost; they barely see him. After three days sitting next to him on a train, they would have difficulty giving evidence as to his appearance, let alone his identity. Others watch him from the corners of their eyes and daydream his possible lives, where he's come from, where he's going all alone. Can he really be as young as he looks?

On the second or third day, another young man breaks the ice with Brian as they stand together in the wind in the small space at the end of the carriage, by offering him a cigarette which, although not being a confirmed smoker, he accepts. Some mysterious connection has apparently brought them together, because the other man, or boy, whose name we shall say is Peter, reveals that, by strange coincidence, he, too, is on his way to begin training at the naval base at Crib Point. His and Brian's paths had not already crossed at the navy recruiting centre in Perth only because, immediately before his departure from the West, Peter had been given leave to help with the annual harvest on his parents' wheat farm outside Katanning, south of Perth.

'I grew up on a farm, too,' says Brian, dizzy from the tobacco. 'Until I was six. Near Kirk's Rock, east of Yealering.'

If you consult an atlas, you will find Yealering lies on the Narrogin–Merredin road, 200-or-so kilometres south-east of Perth, more east than south. Unless your map is highly detailed, you're unlikely to locate Kirk's Rock itself, so will be left to presume it's to be found somewhere in the blank space circumscribed by the alliterative farming towns of Kulin, Kondinin, and Corrigin — perhaps there, where the fine red line of a minor road crooks and heads north. Peter, coming from 150 kilometres further south, knows the district only vaguely, it not being somewhere you'd be likely to visit, or even pass through, without specific reason.

'Then the bank took the farm off us, and we moved to the city.' Brian remembers his earliest days on the farm as a kind of paradise. Roaming about with the sheep and the chooks and the cow for milking, building dams across the tiny creek in winter, when the rains had blown through and the paddocks greened. His first school was there, in the salmon gums, one room with a bell and a flag and a map of the world with Greenland stretching forever (and not green at all) and, on the cold days, a fire crackling in the wood-heater by Miss Henry's desk. On the shelf behind her lay a row of books that seemed to contain clues to all the world's great secrets, from Mississippi paddle-steamers to the ancient pyramids of Egypt.

As often happens when peers first meet, the two 17-year-olds on the train exchange biographical information, and so map out their lines of similarity and difference. Whereas Brian had been a scholarship boy at Perth Modern School, Peter had been sent to boarding school, one of those well-off colleges where you learnt rugby and rowing and easy confidence. Against Brian's three younger brothers, Peter contrasts two sisters, one older, one younger. Where Brian's first choice was always the navy, to begin with, Peter had applied unsuccessfully to be a fighter pilot in the Royal Australian Air Force.

They play chess together on a table in the dining car, and find themselves competitively matched. Peter, the more worldly of the pair, and somewhat better resourced, shares his cigarettes and, in the evening, brings over a bottle of beer he has purchased at the bar. The brown curve of the bottle, the smell of the beer, its bitter taste, remind Brian once more of his father.

The lounge car at night, into which he'd never previously ventured, is swathed in smoke and giddy with drunkenness. Women sit, cigarettes in hand, upon the laps of men. Mouths are open wide with jokes and laughter, so you can see whose teeth are rotten or filled with mercury.

The boy ingénues raise their eyebrows at each other and watch, out of the corners of their eyes, here a hand that wanders along a hemline or clasps clumsily to a blouse, there an open-mouthed, lipstick-smeared kiss. This is the forbidden world of the Barrack Street front bars, past which Brian's mother would quickly pull the children on their way home from the cinema on a late Saturday afternoon, glimpsed briefly as the saloon door swung open to eject a drunken troublemaker.

Someone has persuaded one of the guards to unlock the

lid of the piano at the far end, and is rolling out some popular favourites with more gusto than finesse. The whole carriage joins in on the choruses: 'There'll be bluebirds over/the white cliffs of Dover', rocking from side to side and giggling.

The blinds are pulled down tight for blackout at night as the train snakes through the wartime countryside. Peter has struck up a conversation with a girl and pours more beer, which Brian drinks until, quite suddenly, the hazy, exotic spectacle of pleasure turns greenish and Brian is aware that he can no longer breathe or hold the contents of his stomach down. The noise of the carriage swirls in his head with the rhythmic swaying of the train, and he feels himself disappearing down a distant plughole, while at the same time desperately trying to stop what he can feel headed up the other way. He needs fresh air. He should go out of the carriage, find his way to the toilet. He vomits on the floor and on Peter's leg.

The next morning, as the train finally approaches Melbourne, they make light of the incident and their hangovers. Brian is relieved that Peter is not intent on furthering his humiliation. 'You need to learn how to hold your drink, son,' he hears his father bark at him. 'What did you think you were doing in there at your age?' whispers his mother, 'Anything could have happened — you could have been robbed!' Brian feels for his wallet in the pocket of his trousers. As he moves around the train, he tries to avoid eye contact with anyone he recognises from the night before.

'How're you feeling? You feeling better?' It's the nice woman who had helped clean him up. 'Gotta watch out with trains; it's the motion,' she says. 'Mind you, it's good for sleeping, I had a good sleep last night until all that noise in Ararat. You joining up, are you? I'm in the WAAF. They say the war's going to be over before we know it.'

Brian watches the endless factories and cottages and busy streets of Melbourne's western suburbs roll by. Smoke and steam rise from chimneys in all directions, their various plumes coalescing in a grey-brown ceiling hitched below the sky. This is a real city: vast, dirty, and unknowable.

He and Peter have the same instructions: to wait on the platform at Finders Street Station to be met by an officer from the navy. Families and friends reunite around them, with hugs and tears and 'look at you's. Passengers on their own struggle by with luggage, craning necks to locate a familiar face, or just a way out. A hawker is calling out for business, selling cigarettes and lollies, while down the way a newsstand does brisk trade.

Gradually, the crowd thins — people melt away up the stairs at one end of the platform or down at the other — so that it is easy to notice the crisply uniformed figure skittering down the stairs and towards them.

It turns out there are another three naval recruits from the west waiting on the platform. Had they travelled on distant carriages? The five of them, with their bags by their feet, stand together on the platform as the officer wanders up and down and confers with the guard, evidently comparing lists of names. Eventually, he comes across to speak to them.

'One of you is missing,' he says. 'We were expecting six.' He says it as if he may hold them all collectively responsible for the loss of this final member of their party.

Petty Officer Bennett proceeds to call a roll of those present, from which he deduces that it is the recruit Holditch, D. who is missing. Having established that none of the others know Holditch, D., he tells them to remain exactly where they are until he has made absolutely certain that said Holditch, D. was not travelling on the train. He needs to do everything necessary to ensure *he* cannot be blamed by the powers that be for the disappearance or misplacement of said recruit.

Brian casts his mind back to the desert station, where he imagines Holditch, D., heady with the romance of the landscape, slipping out from the clamour of the crowd to behind the station wall, there to wait until the train has resumed its passage east. However, his intentions from there, Brian finds, are difficult to fathom. Perhaps he is merely homesick and wants to await the next train west. Perhaps he is gone mad and plans to walk into the desert to meet God.

Petty Officer Bennett is back, apparently satisfied that he's done enough. 'Follow me,' he says, and takes his polished black shoes back up the stairs.

❧

There is a real Peter. His name is Peter Graham, and he served with my father from 1945 until demobilisation in 1947.

I met him in Perth in 1995 at his house in Nedlands, where I learnt he didn't meet Brian on the train at all; rather, they were friends at Perth Modern School before they joined the navy. It occurred to me that Brian might have taken a ship across the Great Australian Bight instead of a train to Melbourne — the records I had seen weren't clear. If so, this would dissolve at a stroke the backdrops I had grown so fond of. I decided I couldn't bear for him to go back now, and come another way. Train or ship; it was the journey that mattered.

The real Peter was gentle and courteous and not at all reminiscent of rugby players, unlike his namesake on my train, who is big and broad-shouldered, like a friend of mine from childhood, Simon.

I used to stay overnight at Simon's place, and go on holidays with his family, which to me, at the time, seemed perfect. He had a mother and a father, both young and attractive, and two younger sisters, the baby adorably cute. His parents would even drink wine poured from a cask at an ordinary dinner at home, a practice I found intriguingly decadent.

His mother was slim and blonde-haired, a zoologist studying quokkas, those squat little marsupials extinct on the Australian mainland but familiar to Western Australians as residents of tiny Rottnest Island, just off Perth, where they droop beside the kitchen steps of holiday bungalows, begging for scraps of lettuce or other food. I remember that I got on particularly well with her; she had a lively sense of humour.

Simon's father was muscular and nuggety, with a thick black beard; he was a rheumatologist. Later on, by one of those coincidences that happen in a small town like Perth, his father treated the ankylosing spondylitis that my sister suffered from in her final year of school. I had less experience, of course, in relating to fathers, which may be why I found him more remote and intimidating than his wife, although an active, dynamic figure who could be great fun.

They had a Kombi campervan, in which I joined them on at least one long holiday touring the south-west of Western Australia. Simon and I slept in a little tent, while the rest of them had berths in the van itself. We must have been about 12 at the time. I remember the two of us sitting up by torchlight and reading pornographic fiction that had somehow fallen into our hands.

Living with Simon's family, I felt an overwhelming sense of comfort and security. His parents were luminous Greek gods in 1970s garb, leading their three golden-haired children safely home from Kombi odysseys. Their nuclear intactness I found alluring and seductive. (It was unsettling, not so many years later, to hear that the parents had divorced. It was then I realised that the roles they had played in my own midsummer night's dream, where all lovers are reunited in the end, belied another, subtler tale.)

One day, I would be reunited with my father. If I waited patiently and was good, he would come back. And he would tell me what to do. He would know things, as fathers should, and he would lead me, as fathers do. He would make me complete and enable me to begin my real life. Until then, I must wait, patiently. Such were the faultlines of my desire. Why should I accept his absence if, in my experience, he was never there to begin with?

သ

He is unfathomable. I can never reach him. But look! Here he is now, emerging into the light at Flinders Street Station early that morning in 1945.

Did we decide he was wearing his uniform already? Melbourne at street level is even louder than on the platforms below. Streets grinding with trams, crowded with swarming office men, hats buzzing up and down the pavements …

Brian stands in the Melbourne street buffeted by the smell and noise of the city. It is January 1945, and he faces at least six months of training at HMAS *Cerberus* before being sent on active duty. By this time, the war will be over, although the troops will not be demobilised until early 1947.

During and beyond his time of service, Brian will develop scattered symptoms that have the military doctors groping for diagnoses. By September 1948, the deputy commissioner of the Repatriation Commission, Mr C. Taylor, will write to advise that, after full consideration of all the evidence available, the Repatriation Board has accepted Able Seaman Carlin's 'NERVOUS CONDITION' as being due to war service.

At first, this appears to be a conundrum: how can said 'NERVOUS CONDITION' be due to service in a war already over before he commenced duty? Brian will never experience any of the catalogue of wartime horrors one might imagine: his ship won't be strafed by bombers nor shadowed by deadly submarines; nor will he be forced to look an enemy in the eye as he bayonets him, the instant before he himself is bayoneted; nor face the nightmares of the Burma Road or Changi. He will never experience starvation, torture, or shellshock.

So — what? What will take place in these two years of service, after the Japanese surrender but before the official declaration of peace, that will so disturb him, mind and body? Could it be, simply, the effects of loneliness, far from home and family? Or could there be, despite the absence of the Japanese, just one day, one hour, one moment that makes him susceptible forever after to the dangerous whisper of madness? A primal scene of such searing horror that it brands him deep within his skin, so that he can never escape the crackling stench?

❦

Last night, I dreamt of crocodiles. I was walking with a party along a path leading past rivers and bays. Near every enticingly cool stretch of water we feared these predators, who would run and snap at us at any chance, and chase us into a hasty retreat.

Finally, I was alone, and the path broadened up a wooded hill, across which streamed hundreds of crocodiles, wakened from their midday snoozing in the bushes and lumbering down towards the water to our left. They marched in parallel, intent on their destination, which was the only thing that would save me, if I could find a way to skip lightly through their ranks without distracting them.

This week, under a dark-grey sky, the crocodiles have been roaming. Should I bring a gun next time? What are the proper uses of guns?

❦

If one is tempted to indulge in forbidden pleasures, one must pay the price in violent pain. Is this what my father believed? But what forbidden pleasures?

I remember now: I haven't told you yet about the gun. My mother said: 'There was a gun.' This was her way of telling us the secret. I was 14, my sister twenty. We sat in a sunny office belonging to Dr Hugh Cook, our well-loved and reliable family GP who, uncannily it always seemed to me, had recently undertaken further training to become a psychiatrist. It was as if he had metamorphosed especially to fit our needs.

I was only dimly aware of the events that led up to the meeting that day. Wendy, I realised much later, already knew something of the story — the revelation had triggered a kind of nervous collapse, which Dr Cook was treating. I remember Wendy had moved out of home to stay with an older couple that she was friends with; but, apart from that, there are only fleeting shadows, vague sensations of unease.

With my brother, John, overseas on a post-university backpacking adventure, Dr Cook called my sister, mother, and me together that day for a family conference, a forum in which my mother would be able to tell, at last, the story of what had happened to Brian.

'He went to a farm, and there was a gun there,' she said, with tears streaming down her face. This was as close as she could go to the word 'suicide'. Her story was extremely short, as short as possible, it seemed, as if she was clinging to the edge of a cliff and every further word might send her toppling over. He had suffered a mental illness and, although he was often well and happy and loved us all dearly, it had eventually led him to — the gun.

I remember very clearly that, although the revelation of suicide came as no surprise to me, the surprise was that I had never once in my 14 years thought of it before. How clever is the mind to play such tricks, to be able to hide from itself even what is in plain view? A strict etiquette applies, it seems: the words themselves must be enunciated before the thoughts may surface from their vaults in the unconscious. I was impressed by my shattering blindness. I wasn't shocked or horrified, except by how much it clearly upset my mother to talk of it. I felt perversely proud to be able to claim such an impossibly tragic history as my own. My father committed suicide before I even knew him! What a card to have been dealt! What a dramatic banner headline! I felt like scrawling it on walls.

This day was the culmination of Wendy's treatment. Our little gathering, with the afternoon sunlight streaming in through the windows, signified the end of her time of sickness, in which a seemingly unrelated accumulation of complaints had, over several years, afflicted first her back, then her knees, and finally her mind. After that day, having participated in the ritual of the talking cure, we all went home and didn't mention any of it again.

❧

In the meantime, I have left Brian there on Flinders Street, thin and teetering at the dawn of his adult life, becoming more and more wraithlike as he awaits his destiny.

At 17, we think the universe is possible. At that age, I believed I might invent a new philosophy that had the power to change the world. It would tie together all the threads I had gathered from reading Sartre, Kafka, and Dostoevsky, and from absorbing the student radicalism of my elder siblings, with their environmental and anti-nuclear-action groups, and it would supplant Marxism as the revolutionary hope of the future. In time, it might come to be known as 'Carlinism', and it would constitute a cure for all social ills, a new, unquenchable light on the hill, ample compensation for any sins that I might be guilty of.

What about Brian? What are his extravagant dreams at seventeen? Is he hoping to prove to his father that he can perform nobly in the navy, and thereby at last win his respect and love, or else gain the strength, like Oedipus, to kill him — and, in either case, in so doing, shed his callow, childish shell to emerge triumphant, reborn as a Man?

Chapter Three

My sister, Wendy, called last night from England. She remembers having come to Perth to stay for months with Brian's mother, Doris, our Gran, at Scarborough in 1963, while Brian was in hospital. She would have been six at the time.

Scarborough was then a quiet seaside suburb, a few dotted rows of housing reaching out into the scrubby sand dunes. Wendy remembers the huge billboard advertising *Lawrence of Arabia* on the flat road into Scarborough. And the first Kennedy death: a tall, fat headline on the newspaper that Mum left lying on the front seat of the car while she went to buy a Choc-Wedge. A scorching day, the ocean glassy, not a whiff yet of the sea breeze. *Are these the sand dunes he stumbles through, the car he leaves parked by the beach?*

Wendy hated having to go to school in Perth uprooted from

her friends. The teacher terrified her. She made fun of Wendy in front of the whole class for assuming the letters in 'Wednesday' would follow the pattern of those in her own name: 'Wendsday'.

One night at Gran's, she remembers, a night when Brian must have been home on weekend leave from the hospital, she overheard Brian and our mother, Joan, talking to Gran. There was some very difficult decision to be made. The television was on, they assumed we weren't listening, Wendy said. There was *all this* discussion about lobotomy — or electric shock? It was a dangerous thing to do to her father's head, this much was clear, and nobody knew quite what would happen, or what *should* happen. And somehow the conversation also became jumbled in her mind with a boxing match she had watched on TV in which someone seemed to die from getting smacked on the head.

Wendy snuck a box of matches from the kitchen and locked herself in the toilet. It may have been the 'boxing match' that led her sideways to this idea. She needed to test a theory she had developed that, if she dropped the box of matches on her head, counted to five, and waited, she would die. She sat there on the cold seat, terrified, looking at the back of the toilet door and summoning the courage.

There she is, in the memory we embroider: on the toilet, with her arm stretched up, the box of matches suspended high above her head, and her heart jumping back and forth against her ribs, thinking she is about to die. She drops the box. It tumbles onto her forehead and off her shoulder onto the floor. Good enough for a direct hit. She makes the count: one, two, three, four … five. She holds her breath. Through the walls and the door, she can hear the faint sound of the TV and the adults murmuring. A moth camps in a high corner, near the coastline of a water stain.

Nothing like death appears to happen. She has a wee and wipes her bottom. No one sees her slip the matches back onto the stove. Perhaps she has saved him: has she not proven these things won't kill him? If that stupid teacher could only see the things she could really do! She returns to the *Wonderful World of Disney*, and wonders whether dessert is still a chance.

My brother, John, who lives a lot closer to me now than Wendy (a suburb away), had just turned eight when Brian died. His birthday was celebrated only days before. He claims not to remember much at all of anything from his early childhood. Forgetfulness, a consoling blanket. Later, I will ask him to remember more and see what happens.

℘

Growing up, it seemed we came from nowhere. There were no stories told of what came before, or of how we got here. I sometimes envy writers who talk about the storytellers in their families, the rich oral traditions maintained by their grandmothers, their great-uncles. They who sat around under ancient trees in Latin courtyards or on summer porches and breathed life into strange tales and larger-than-life characters from times going a-way-way back.

For us, we had the ticking, in the quiet, of the grandfather clock on the mantel. Regular and circumspect. The past was a damp and unhealthy place, full of shadows and darkness. What good could come of looking there? This, it seemed, was not just a matter for my family, with our particular secrets, but permeated the uneasy conscience of our fellow citizens-at-large, who had only recently deigned to admit into their ranks the infinitely disturbing and reviled *Aborigines* of the country.

We never knew *Aborigines* as children. We knew normal people who were white people, and we knew explorers who each had their own snail-trails across the maps of Australia hung with dowel and string on the walls of our classrooms. Sturt: blue dot-dot-dash; Leichhardt: red dash-dash; Stuart: purple dot-dash-dot. I liked the crisscross patterns that their journeys made. It was like some crazy running race where everyone starts from somewhere different and ends up going around in circles and falling over in the sun. It inspired me to draw my own imaginary continents with my own explorers dash-dash-dotting. Would they find the treasure?

The one time that *Aborigines* came crashing into our Perth childhood, a car shot over the hill by our house in Haldane Street, Mount Claremont, very nearly airborne as it flew across the Mayfair Street T-junction and rolled over and over down the slope into the Alnutts' place (before it was the Alnutts' place), smashing through the lounge-room glass. It is a scene for which I have no independent witnesses, no one to help reassemble its riches. But, as lodged in the memory of a six-year-old Aussie WASP brought up with golliwogs and Little Black Sambo, this is how it appeared. Five, ten (20?) black bodies tumbled out of the car, ran away down the side path and along the back lane, to vanish by the bus stop, leaving only the wreck and an abrupt silence. The magpies watched from the gum trees, upstaged, as we picked our way home across the prickles.

છ્ય

As I seek to chisel out my father from thin air and search for clues to his unhappiness or madness, I am drawn further back into the family history. I have some papers from my great-uncle, Ben Carlin, brother of Brian's father, Tom, which I collected around the time of Ben's death, when my mother had the job of cleaning out his flat in Cottesloe.

The papers lie in a manila folder, grimy with handling, stained by coffee and the rubbed imprints of carbon paper. He has jotted stray numbers on the back. On the raised tab, a single word scrawled in pencil: 'TREE'.

Inside the folder, I find an aerogramme addressed to Ben from a Miss Muriel Swires, the archivist at Pateley Bridge, Harrogate, in Yorkshire, May 1962. Miss Swires told Ben that she had searched the parish registers in vain for a record of the birth of a William Carlin, tailor, occurring during any year from 1551, when records presumably began, until 1806. I picture Ben receiving the letter: he scowls, puts his muddy boots up on his desk, and lights a cigarette.

Uncle Ben, as we called him, was a man's man. At the end of his life, he washed up home to Western Australia to die, after conquering the big bad world beyond. I met him then. Like John Wayne in *The Searchers*, he rode in from the wilderness to the homestead, large against the sky and bearing the weight of everything he'd seen and done. He shacked up in a little flat in Overton Gardens, Cottesloe, halfway up a hill, above the Indian Ocean.

It was absurd. This grizzle-jawed urban cowboy ex-journalist; ex-Washington, DC, cab driver; ex-major in the Indian army; thrice married and just as divorced; *ex-goddamned circumnavigator of the planet in an amphibious jeep, if you don't mind, and if you don't believe me, here's the picture they published in* Time *magazine, that's the jeep on the Hudson River, 'Half-Safe' she was called, and that's the goddamned steel cliffs of the Queen Mary towering behind her* — and here he was, cooped up like a *pensioner* (he would spit out the word, as if an insect on his tongue). It's a wonder that he fitted through the front door.

'Perth', he grunted. A decent beer, Emu Bitter: about the only thing you could say for the place. He came over one summer to our house in Haldane Street to fix a kitchen cupboard, swaggering in with a cardboard box of longneck Emus under his arm. It was only Mum and me there; with me at 13 years old and Mum never one to have much more than a glass, it was obvious that he was planning to drink a fair bit himself.

He was scary — the way big, strong men *were* scary. They were a foreign species, initiates of a different realm. They knew things and did things that I couldn't fathom. They talked rough, made crude jokes. At any moment, they might grab you by the scruff of the neck and eyeball you. Like schoolyard bullies. *You wanna go? Come on then. You wanna go?* They had balls. They weren't afraid to fight.

I once stole a cigarette, for no particular reason, from an older boy on a school camp. I didn't smoke. I tried a few times over the years, but was unable to escape the fact that it tasted disgusting and made me dizzy.

Stealing a cigarette was simply the sort of thing you needed to do at 14 on a school camp at an all-boys school, unless you were a wuss, a poof, a fag.

Afterwards, I allowed the older boy to terrorise me for a year. Whenever I was walking in the schoolyard, I looked for him at the next corner. He never did anything more than threaten and act tough, but that was enough to keep me scared — not scared like I was always thinking about it, but back-of-the-mind scared.

UNCLE BEN LASTED a few years in Cottesloe before a series of strokes slammed him into hospital. Mum and I were the only relatives with whom he hadn't fallen out: me, because I was still too young; and Mum, because she maintained good relations with all the Carlins, no matter what they did. She could always see their side. Ben wouldn't speak to Brian's brothers, Eric, Noel, and Andrew, in each case because of some altercation years before in which they had disagreed with his advice. Latterly, even my long-haired uni-student brother John had upset him.

At the end, we visited him over in South Perth, in the hospital or aged-care home or whatever it was that he was stuck in. He gave me an ugly gold digital watch that sat chunky on my wrist. Later, I accidentally smashed it playing hockey. The most recent stroke had taken away his voice. He was reduced to sitting up in bed and pounding with his finger on a primitive portable device designed to display what he could no longer say.

The machine absorbed all the determination of his frozen-up body. All the fury in his eyes was squeezed through his fingertip into the bland binaries of Atari-land: 'Fuck this.' He twisted the writing board towards us, and his face into a savage grin. That was the last time I ever saw him. He ordered that his ashes be scattered to the winds.

IN HIS GENEALOGICAL PHASE, Uncle Ben discovered ancestors who were hatters and tobacconists in London in the early-19th century.

Born in 1819 and apprenticed to a Westminster vintner was one Frederick Benjamin Carlin, who, Uncle Ben scrawled drily in the margins, 'eloped with the boss's daughter Sarah'.

Let's say it's true … an impossible, illicit love, blossomed from a first encounter between scrawny shop-boy and well-scrubbed will-o'-the-wisp girl, hemmed into her best Sunday petticoats as if in a penny dreadful. But their future, alas for romance, was to be highly respectable: they married and emigrated to South Australia, the new society of free settlers, where they were 'attracted by the possibilities for hardware business'. This in the words of the family's other historian, Brian's brother Eric, who now steps, or is dragged, into my story.

Eric, in his retirement, has spent time, in between golf, travel, and other pursuits, researching a manuscript entitled 'Our Family Forebears'. Where Uncle Ben dabbled in family history on quiet evenings in between adventures, Eric set out in a more methodical, scholarly fashion, befitting his former profession as a lecturer in teacher training.

Some years ago, I visited Eric and Alison at their new house in Perth in the carpet-lawned suburb of St John's Wood, where a developer's vision of suburban perfection had been laid out over the sand-dune country of the old Graylands asylum.

Eric took me into his study and showed me the old photographs, family letters, and other documents that he had collected and archived over the years. He brought out one of his most treasured possessions, a walking stick carved from red gum by the famed explorer John McDouall Stuart, the first white man to cross Australia *south to north and back* (of those maps: purple dot-dash-dot), and friend of another forebear, John Sinclair, whose family married into the Carlins.

Since Brian's death, Eric, as the next eldest brother, had assumed a role as the family patriarch. Long before I dared broach the subject of Brian with my mother, I wrote to Eric, from the other side of the continent and in some trepidation. I half-expected a cold and chiding riposte requesting I desist from bringing up such a *shameful* issue. I was hugely relieved to find a richly generous 12-page reply in the mail one day, written in tight, fine hand on soft and silky air-letter paper. How I savoured the feel of that paper in my hand!

Dear David,
I was surprised but very pleased to have your letter today ...

I like the way he says 'have your letter' — such an old-fashioned turn of phrase, harking back to the grandest days of letter-writing: prepare yourself for the pleasures of a lengthy epistle, my dear nephew ...

Actually, I find myself now with many Erics here, none of whom should be assumed to coincide with the existing person of that name, who was, and is, the brother of my father:

I have the gentle, loving Eric in his personal letter, penned in flowing longhand, chronicler of a story he has waited 30 years to tell me, a story only he *can* tell; this Eric whose confidences I betray.

I have the public, word-processed (with help from his daughter) Eric of 'Our Family Forebears', writing for posterity, the historical record, and whomsoever may be interested, seeking to lay down the facts as objectively as possible, rational, impartial.

And then I have the shifting, multifaceted Eric of my memories, both recent and long ago: the jolly Eric of my childhood, singing silly songs to my cousin and me as we bounced along, seatbelt-less, in his old Kingswood, past Perry Lakes; the tall uncle in his shorts, his hair already thinning, drinking longneck beers and talking politics over the barbecue, or returning from a morning jog or swim; and now, the stooping older man, ever-more conscious of his mortality, still tall and knobbly-kneed in the late sun at his beach house, but arching forward to better lip-read on account of his bad ears, still with that tinder-dry wit exploding into guffawing laughter.

Before telling me about Brian, Eric says, across the lightness of the paper, 'I think it may be helpful if we go back a bit.' The first Eric beckons me towards the second. To know Brian, I should understand the family he came from.

But, as it is a long and ragged story, I will trim it. Everyone knows slideshows are boring. So I will leave out the French fiddler who jumped ship in Albany in the early days and hid out at the vicar's place seducing the vicar's daughter; I will leave out Papa Tondut, who planted the first grapevines in South Perth and entertained the governor on the latter's Sunday horserides — you see, already the second one is less interesting than the first.

Our first slide (pay attention and there will be supper): great-great-great-grandfather Frederick Benjamin and equally great Sarah (they who had eloped, in Ben's opinion), arriving at Port Adelaide towards the end of 1847, in the 11th year of that settlement promoted as an oasis of decency and civilisation in the colonial wilderness. Much rigging and bustle in the background, as they step off the ship.

Now, here, the grand hardware store they built in Rundle Street; here, Frederick the esteemed burgher elected local mayor (note the impressive beard). Here (moving quickly), their son William marrying Isabella Sinclair and, in 1896, taking his family westward (another boat scene) to Captain Stirling's 'Hesperia', the vastly disappointing Swan River colony latterly reborn, almost overnight, with the discovery of gold.

While the rest of Australia languished in depression, Perth was flush with hope. Men from the eastern states streamed into Fremantle and on towards the goldfields of Kalgoorlie and Coolgardie. Investment capital flowed in from London. Afghans and their camel teams floated eastward into the desert like mirages. Tent cities sprouted along the river flats of the Swan, where the civic council's beautification schemes could not keep pace.

The Carlins disembarked into the noise and bustle of Fremantle — a town, according to historian F. K. Crowley, 'covered in fine white dust and dominated by a large prison, a lunatic asylum, and a hospital for decrepit convicts'. There they lived for several years before making their way north along the crowded highway towards the capital, having gathered the resources to secure a block of land in the promising suburb of West Leederville. (Family posed in formal clothes on square of sand in blazing sun. Eldest son, Frederick Cecil, born 1876, steps forward.)

Frederick Cecil is the first ancestor to emerge from history into living memory, as Eric's (and Brian's) grandfather. It was he who sired the fateful trio, the legendary monstrous siblings: Tom, Jess, and Ben.

The eldest, Brian's father, Tom (christened thus, it appears, without further adornment, like a pug); the infamous and much-feared Jess Bramwell who, although twice married, never brought forth children (this, no doubt, held against her); and, eight years later, an afterthought or accident, the second and much doted-upon Frederick Benjamin, Uncle Ben.

I picture the three of them, all dead now 20 years or more, sitting across the middle of the family tree like hanging judges at the bench, or gargoyles in a row. Whatever have they done to deserve these caricatures? It must be the stories whispered by those who've lived to tell the tale.

Frederick Cecil, apprenticed in railway electrics, spent 42 years with the Western Australian Government Railways, rising through the ranks to the position of chief electrical inspector.

On his final day in 1940, his boss presented him with a world-range Philips radio which, as reported in the next issue of *Western Australian Railway and Tramway* magazine, F. C. received with thanks, no regrets, and the wish that, in this time of war, 'the radio would bring good tidings of world affairs'. Hear, hear, the audience rumbled (unreported). Reading further in the same month's *Railway and Tramway*, one could take succour from these words of advice, penned anonymously: 'I've shut the door on yesterday and thrown away the key. To-morrow holds no doubt for me since I have found to-day.'

Things were simple, strong, and manly in the railways: lines parallel, gradients measured, curves kept to a discreet minimum, clear and unambiguous signals (Frederick's division) regulating behaviour. It had to be so; the slightest buckling of those parameters and the whole system would convulse, spewing metal and sparks.

These principles, it would appear, Frederick also applied at home. No buckling.

A photo shows Brian's grandmother, Charlotte, or 'Lovey' as she was known, posed in a studio on her wedding day, standing beside Frederick, who is seated in a cane chair. She is tiny, her skinny waist and arms wrapped tight in the long, white gown of the day, her gloved right hand seeming to hover uncertainly just above the arm of her elegantly moustachioed husband's chair. Here, her face, above the high, white collar, shines young and bright, her gaze strong, the slightest hint of a smile enlivening the line of her lips. Something there reminds me of my sister. But Lovey was sickly and died young of a bad heart, leaving

Frederick to take care of the three children, Tom, Jess, and Ben.

Eric reads to me a letter Lovey wrote to an adolescent Tom as he returned home with his four-year-old brother from a visit to their aunt. The letter is dated three weeks before she died: it sounds now as an elegy. Propped up in bed, scratching at the words, whispering towards the dark: 'Take care of Ben coming down, son. Don't get out of the carriage and leave him alone. Be sure to keep him warm. It was so nice to hear that you were so kind to Baby. It was raining again today ...'

The rain, not gentle and dreary as in English books but pounding, brief and fresh from the Indian Ocean, to be drunk up by the sand, thankful when it comes.

Chapter Four

My father was Frank Sinatra. My sister saw him at the age of nine on the big screen at the Grand on Murray Street, where they had the armrests and the choc-tops. Not just any Frank Sinatra: the hero in *Von Ryan's Express*. The man they called Von Ryan who, leather-jacketed and bandage-faced, led a great escape of POWs from the Nazis on a prison train through Italy, via Hollywood: wasn't that Brian, her dad, who'd been away to the Second World War and fought and — somehow — died? Didn't she remember him looking just so tall and handsome?

When the real war still raged, Brian's grandfather, Frederick Cecil, who did not yet know how short-lived a retirement he would have before the cancer swamped his prostate, sat in his dark wood-panelled house in Perth's West Leederville, and wound the dials on his new radio to hear the solemn chimes of Big Ben ring out across the neatly tended buffalo.

The wireless carried no news, of course, of his own *brave fighting sons*, Tom and Ben; the first, the family man, helping lead the fight at home, working slowly up the career-soldier ranks to Warrant Officer; the second, the cavalier youngest child, blustering and charming his way to instant elevation to Major with the British Indian Army on the strength of his largely untested skills as an engineer.

(How on earth did Ben end up in India? The story goes that he had arrived there overland from Shanghai, where he had been holed up for some months drinking cocktails, courtesy of a salaried position he enjoyed at a mine elsewhere in China to which the outbreak of war had prevented his reporting for duty.) But Frederick, already on his deathbed by 1942, did at least receive word from Ben to say that he was still alive and touring jauntily towards Palestine.

He started to reply, in a letter Eric showed me. Frederick's voice, fragile now, a kiss of wind across a marshland:

Jess was beginning to think you'd gone west. I clung to the belief that we'd hear from you, more to cheer Jess, I think … You certainly are having a good look-see and I would certainly like the opportunity to see all the storied spots of which you are in the midst …

Auntie Jess, Frederick Cecil's mercurial only daughter, looked after him at the end in the dark house and the hospital, as she had done all the years since Lovey's death, save briefly when her father remarried and Jess experimented with a short-lived marriage of her own in Sydney. (It turned out that Frederick's second wife was, sadly, no better a survivor than the first. Jess's husband didn't expire, but their marriage did, and she retreated home to her father for the duration.)

Of Jess and Frederick's relationship, Eric says, poker-faced: 'Now that's the facts, you can read whatever you like into it.'

Whatever the Oedipal overtones, Jess was a kettle of fish, that's to be sure. In Perth in the 1920s, for a smart girl with a university education, opportunities were few. She was to spend all her working life at the firm of Brown & Dureau, import agents in the city. Keeping their books.

Brown & Dureau brought to the citizens of Perth many of life's essentials and a good few of its luxuries; it was the sort of town where you always had to order things from somewhere else. Jess, scanning the details of each consignment, savoured the sophisticated whiff of its origin, the glow of the names upon the page … New York, Marseilles, Liverpool, Cape Town. These were places that you read about in books, glimpsed in movies. She deserved better, in her opinion.

As a Carlin, she deserved better. If only she were a man, like her beloved younger brother, gallivanting here and there.

In lieu of conventional means of transport, she acquired a great love of alcohol, or at least a respect for what it could accomplish. In her prime, she could have a whole party hanging on her wit, although later her judgement deserted her and the punchlines failed to match the promise. In middle age, she took to hiding a bottle of sherry and a glass in a cupboard in every room and, I'm told, would circulate through the house, quietly drinking.

Jess could make you nervous. My aunt Alison says that every time she saw a letter arrive in Jess's unmistakable hand, she'd tense for the 'sting in the tail'.

But then, all the Carlins of the generations immediately before my father were famously volcanic. Alison says there was always that feeling with the Carlins that you were sitting on the edge of your chair not quite knowing what was going to happen. Just take Ben: for him, a woman was either *a bloody peach* or *a bloody bitch*, and the slip between was quickly travelled.

Tom's wife, Doris, my Gran Carlin, was terrified of the lot of them her whole life. She'd be frightened if Jess merely called up on the phone. In the early days, I imagine old Frederick Cecil first instilled the fear in Doris over cheerless dinners at his home, correcting her table manners and her grammar. Later, when Tom assumed the head of the table, he carried on the persecution to the great discomfort of his daughters-in-law seated nearby (his sons were more than used to it). He mocked any view or comment that Doris expressed until, in retreating to the kitchen, she found busyness to hide in.

As CHILDREN, we went to Gran's for dinner with all the cousins every Sunday without fail. But we didn't call it dinner, which was some posh thing you'd have in a restaurant; we called it 'tea'.

At the doorstep, as we left for the long drive home through the scrub and dunes where they hadn't filled in the suburbs yet, she handed us a regular block of Cadbury's Milk Chocolate to share. A treat for the week. We rationed it, square by square, each night after tea.

Doris was everything a gran was supposed to be: small, white-haired, cheery, an expert cook of steamed puddings, and not averse to the purchase of malted milkshakes at the Forum café in Hay Street. We sat at the same dinner table in her house that Tom had dominated; but he was long dead now, and a happy chaos disorganised the room, overflowing into the lounge, where Efrem Zimbalist, Jr fired bullets two-handed from the pillarless doors of impossibly American cars.

When Tom died, Doris could breathe at last. That night, for the first time in memory, she didn't feel obliged to scrub and black the stove before slipping into bed. The truth was, cleaning wasn't her thing. She preferred a domestic regime of approximation. The only exception was the washing: it must continue to be boiled up in the copper. She maintained an unshakeable suspicion of washing machines. You can't expect to clean clothes just by *stirring* them. It was important to have crisp, clean sheets; one day, you might die in them (and one day, of course, she did).

Notoriously timid and mousey, Doris joined the Penguin Club for women's public speaking. As if, no longer to be shouted down, she would refine the skill of making people listen.

She discovered that she enjoyed wandering up the hill to put a few bob on the horses on a Saturday morning. Never previously a smoker or a drinker, she took to quietly pouring a tot of whisky into a glass of milk once a day. Let the stove go to buggery — she mightn't say it, but she could taste it in the milk.

But the day Ben turned up unannounced, home suddenly from America after all those years, bursting in at the side-gate with some high-falutin' judge's wife by his side, the shame froze her up again. Never mind it was a day hot enough to droop the camellias, a day to flop in the shade and gaze into the blank, blue sky, waiting for the caress of the sea breeze to touch the branches of the peppermints. What was she thinking, not bothering to dress properly, lounging in her petticoats with the grandchildren?

Alison watched the crimson panic rise in Doris. To have Ben discover her thus, looking like that! Letting herself go! No matter if it's her own backyard; and she has every right, no matter anything she might argue in front of her fellow-Penguins at the local hall, before a nice light supper, the first Tuesday of the month. She scurried inside to get dressed.

No matter what she did, Doris would never quite be good enough for the Carlins.

WEAK MOTHER, overbearing father: a poisonous combination for a young boy growing up. This is a well-known theory of psychology, or so I've been told.

Brian, watching his father and mother together, was confused: is this what a man does? Is this what *I* must do to be a man? This bullying I despise? Because am I not a man? If not a man, what am I?

The depressive's dance, the sing-song hammer of self-harm: what is wrong with me, if I cannot be what I should be?

After the navy, Brian will study Agriculture at university — a choice as solid as any, with new land being opened up and distant memories of the childhood farm lost in the Depression.

But, when the time comes to take an elective and others choose literature or a language, Brian will be drawn like a moth to Psychology. There, he'll fall in with an exotic, bohemian crowd. He'll be exposed to the astonishing wilderness of the mind, journeyed into by Freud and his disciples. A continent of thoughts and impulses beyond our grasp, at the tip of our tongue, beneath our sleeping eyelids — *the unconscious* — from where the barbs and hallucinations brewed up in earliest childhood return and return again to haunt us. Brian will drink in these ideas. And, much later, he will whisper to my mother (so she told me); he will whisper as he tries to impress upon her the heaviness that he feels weighing on him, the story of a scene that he remembers from his own earliest years; and, as he tells her, she can't discern whether what he says is true or a kind of brain-fever of imagining that he suffers — and perhaps he, too, doubts his own mind?

But he does know, yes, he does know what he saw. And Freud has a name for it, which makes it sound mythic, but nevertheless it is *what he saw.*

His father and his mother — you can anticipate what's coming — Brian hears noises through the hessian walls of their farmhouse. He shouldn't be there, he is a naughty boy out of bed in the night; and he (this time, the other 'he') is in the moonlight, hammering himself into her, beating up against her; she is crying out, it is violent and confusing and unforgivable, and Brian feels her pain (if it is pain), but not his father's mastery.

And (because of this, but not just because of this) he feels himself to be a case study for psychology, albeit one that it's not good at solving. As for Joan, with her scant experience of the world, she wonders what on earth she is supposed to do with such a story.

BRIAN'S FATHER, young Tom Carlin, was a handsome catch. Tall and athletic. In his early twenties, he had embarked upon a career with the stock firm Elders that saw him sailing up and down the coast to the vast station country of the Murchison.

He dreamt of leasing his own station and becoming *a man of the land*. The idea left Doris cold. She was a Perth girl who had earned her own living since age 14 in the office of a wholesale grocer in central Hay Street.

Nevertheless, Tom was persuasive and had some money to build upon, left to him by a doting bachelor uncle. By the time Doris and Tom were married, in 1927, he had already taken out a mortgage on a small farm at Cuballing, in the wheat belt. A photograph shows the couple on their honeymoon, en route, motoring 30 miles south from Perth to Rockingham, a modest seaside resort. They perch on the running board of their Model T, side by side, under the heat of the January sun, each chastely clasping his or her own hands in lap and smiling politely for the photographer. Brian would be conceived in Rockingham, and born in Cuballing in October.

No sooner had they settled into the farm at Cuballing than the young family up and moved to one that seemed more promising — the property near Kirk's Rock, out towards the great north–south line of the Rabbit-proof Fence, where Western

Australia had tried in vain to stem the westward flow of feral animals. This is the place that the Brian in my mind remembers as his early home, a tiny weatherboard-and-tin four-roomed house halfway up a rocky rise, with those hessian walls inside. The paddocks of the farm stretched down into the wide, flat valley to where they met with Downies' paddocks at the bottom and the ground rose up again in the distance to the clump of trees around Downies' house. In summer, the east winds off the desert funnelled one way; in winter, the cold fronts barrelled the other.

Tom was determined to make a go of it here, to build himself up, put some money away, one day secure a station, end up lord of a place the size of a small country, like he'd seen up in the Murchison. Doris, the city girl, less than keen, was willing to try her best for him, but within limits. The whispered advice of her sister, also married to a farmer, hung in her ears: 'Whatever you do, never learn to milk.' *It's every morning, every night, come rain or shine, forever. Even with just the one cow. In the dark and the dust and the mud and the flies. You'll have more than enough with trying to keep the house respectable, the kids fed and dressed; don't go mucking in with the farm work.*

The kids: after Brian came the births, in quick succession, of Eric, Noel, and Andrew. Boy after boy after boy after boy — and Doris forever hoping for a girl to share things with. But, once it got to be the Depression, four kids was about all you could hope to feed, so there had to be a stop to trying. Get on with what you have, dear. Make do.

At night, the stars spread thick and peppery. The only noises were the night creatures shuffling in the bush, the wind under the tin. I picture Doris afloat on a great ocean of sadness, drifting alone in her hessian box while Tom snored off the day's exertions. Could there be anyone more alone? A tribe of blacks might swoop in from the trees, and not even the Downies would notice for several days that the Carlin throats had been slit with their own kitchen knives. Had there not been stories of these things? Or was that Africa?

She dreamt of entertaining ladies, of a sweeping drive with curved, stone stairs to meet it. She on the verandah, atop the stairs in her finest hat (that one in the magazine), taking care of her complexion. *How dry the skin becomes! Don't you find? Let's take tea and later walk out into the garden when the sun is kinder* ... sigh. How far away was civilisation! She hungered for its belch and clang, the squealing of the tram wheels as they ground around the corner of William and Hay.

Yealering was the local big smoke, a thriving community, as Tom told her. Children permitting, you could enjoy dances, meetings, and card evenings at Lee's Tea Rooms (Doris scarcely had a chance), and cold beer at the Commercial Hotel (Tom made the effort).

Every Friday, the young couple bundled up Brian and his brothers and travelled the dusty 15-mile journey to town in their Model-A Ford utility named Florence. Eric tells me that his father always carried a brick on the tray because of Florence's temperamental radiator. Halfway up Russell's Hill, without fail, Florence would boil over. Tom would jump out and wedge the brick behind a wheel to stop her rolling back down the hill. And they would wait for the radiator to cool down so they could continue on their way. The children loved Florence, despite her shortcomings, for her ability to take them over the horizon. To the big smoke.

At Yealering, I imagine them stocking up from Mr Kelly at the Farmers Co-op Store, picking up a treat from Mr Parker and that nice Hilda at the bakery, and putting another payment on a new saddle from Bill Honeyman, the harness-maker, who could tell you absolutely everything worth knowing about a horse and plough. But Eric tells me there were no treats that he remembers at Kirk's Rock, only later in Perth (there wasn't the money) and, besides, Doris baked her own bread. Once again, I have to warn you to beware my flights of fancy. Give me an inch and I'll take a mile.

Okay, a new shopping list: flour, tea, sugar. I must be on safer ground there. Everybody had to buy those. But how dull would life be if we could only live on flour, tea, and sugar! I still believe Hilda may have slipped Brian a tiny morsel from the counter once or twice, when Eric wasn't looking. Which would explain, you know. And Tom does need to talk to Bill, picking up wisdom for his farm work. Bill's what we would latterly call a mentor, and I think it would be nice if Tom could have one, since he's all alone at Kirk's Rock, too, just like Doris, only keeping a lid on it more when he talks to himself, and snoring rather than gazing at the ceiling.

One memorable day, a photographer caught Doris with the two eldest boys, Brian and Eric, down by the lake. It was the day Lake Yealering had flooded. In the background, crowds of amused children pick their way along the submerged boards of the town jetty, while men in suits fix their hands upon their hips and look on in amazement. What a lark! Walking on water! Older folks and young mothers sit on the banks behind a row of wicker prams and admire the spectacle.

Doris stands with her back to the lake, in a row of women posing for their picture. One of them licks an ice cream; another wears a jaunty summer scarf tied at the neck above a spotted dress, a curl of hair tickling her nose. But Doris is demure in white. A sensible, wide-brimmed hat protects her from the sun. The moment of the photograph catches her bending forward awkwardly, with a hand outstretched towards little Eric. He won't hold up his head properly for the man, she worries. But it is she who unsettles the composition.

∽

In 1930, Tom wrote a letter home to his father, Frederick Cecil, in West Leederville: 'The boys are growing like mushrooms now and are such characters.' Jess, unearthing the letter among her father's possessions upon his death, cut out, for some reason, a small portion of it to keep: 'Eric is now pulling himself up on anything and everything.' The fragment, upon Jess's death, found its way in turn to Eric: 'The Brian: he is a scream now, with his funny ways and sayings.' And Eric, with his first long, silky air-letter to me, enclosed a photocopy:

The other evening Brian was waltzing around Molly out in the yard with the milk bucket in front of him. 'Don't want any milk tonight Tom, the cow has gone dry.' Only when he is in bad odour or thinks he is, do I get Daddy; when stocks are medium to good it's just plain Tom and no trimmings.

Eric wrote in the margin of the photocopy, simply, quietly, in his study, 'This man I never knew.'

Chapter Five

The lake at Yealering is now, in April, a bare saltpan. Where the waves were are now the rippling tyre tracks of Friday-night adventures. The hoonery of a perfect doughnut.

It is hard to believe that there was so much fresh water here in 1930 that Tom and Doris could watch their neighbours taking pleasure cruises in a launch around the lake.

The locals say, for the record, that if the good rains come in winter you can still go water-skiing, and they point out that, in the old days, sometimes it was so dry the town ran horse races across the salt, and bookmakers lined the jetty. But they will admit that the good rains have been few and far between for quite a while now, and the salt is rising everywhere around the cracking she-oaks. The dusty paddocks see fewer sheep, and the township streets are hollowed out and abandoned, as if all the people have crept away in the night in search of water or — anything, really.

The retreating population has left behind historic boards along the streets to show what used to be. Displayed on hardy metal in a triumph of civic pride: a permanent exhibition of photos and stories of the early days, the days of Tom and Doris, when the empire was still on the march in Western Australia, and districts blossomed along the fresh branches of Frederick Cecil's railway.

But even the boards themselves are looking tired now, unloved and largely ignored. They're built for visitors, but scarcely anybody comes through this way. There are no local attractions worth putting in a brochure. I am the only one interested in salmon gums and dried-up lakes.

In less than 100 years, this outpost of progress has reached its pinnacle and collapsed again, its impatient dreams dashed.

EVEN WHEN BRIAN WAS AN AGRICULTURAL ADVISOR, in the late 1950s and early '60s, there was little or no hint of just how bad conditions would become.

Sitting up late at night, the family asleep and a cigarette burning in the ashtray beneath his desk-lamp, he wrote enthusiastic papers like 'Clearing Sandplain Country' for the *Journal of Agriculture*. He overlaid topographic maps with rainfall data and soil surveys, puzzling how to turn scrubland into productive blocks. But he advised young farmers to be careful setting out.

His words read as a retrospective summation of the mistakes

made by his father, 30 years before, at Kirk's Rock:

> We all know of settlers who have failed because they fell
> short of the mark in relation to one of these three factors …
>   (a) Adequate capital
>   (b) Careful planning
>   (c) Technical 'know-how'

Brian was passionate about bringing science and economics to farmers: they required, he believed, a revolution in their thinking. There was so much that they needed to be on top of: optimum rates of fertiliser per acre, improved pasture management, encouragement of subterranean clover, methods for the development of soils over time, just for example.

Back when he was a little boy, running around the paddocks at Kirk's Rock barefoot and watching his father swear at the horses, farming was just a matter of bending your back and getting on with it.

⌘

Eric has brought me out to Kirk's Rock to see the farm: the first time for me, and for him quite possibly the last. It's a two-and-a-half hour drive south-east from Perth, over the escarpment and into the expanses of the wheat belt. Uncle Noel, Brian's second brother after Eric, sits in the back, irascible, moon-faced. Eric has invited Noel along for the daytrip.

Eric says it's funny how the memories come flooding back

the closer we get to our destination. Noel quietens down, stops talking about the Labor government.

We pause in Yealering for directions. It is a Sunday afternoon, and the town gives every impression of having been recently evacuated. Presumably, the citizens are burrowed deep within their houses; it is hard to find a single soul outdoors.

Finally, we see a man sitting in the shade of his front verandah. He is happy to amble down his front path to chat with Eric at the letterbox while his dog sniffs at the car. The man points up the road and wiggles his finger this way and that, and Eric nods.

Driving off, we come to a place from where we realise the man's directions can be interpreted in either of two ways, and it is only after we pursue one of these options for several kilometres that the three of us agree it must be wrong. Eric does a U-turn in the dirt, and we slide back along our tracks. It is hard to read this country.

We locate a turn-off that Eric thinks may be familiar, and take it. The clouds are woolly polka dots all across the sky. 'This'd have to be Russell's Hill, I reckon,' says Eric, observing some nuance in the landscape that escapes me.

Noel concurs from the back seat, looking out the window: 'Yep, this'd be Russell's Hill alright.'

The country is so flat around these parts that the most gentle and insignificant rises are bestowed the honour of being hills. Florence must have been a delicate vehicle.

We reach the farm. There are few signs of former habitation; a windmill bumps in the breeze above a crumbling concrete watertank. Eric parks the car so we can walk up to the house site. Noel doesn't even get out. Maybe his walking's not so good, but I wonder at his lack of curiosity. Wasn't this the whole point of the trip?

Eric leads me up the slope through the dry grass. He searches for any trace of the house itself. He wanders around, wheels in circles, surveys the horizon: 'It might have been here, I think, but I'm really not sure.' There are no identifying features to get a bearing on. The flies buzz incessantly in our faces, my hand a windscreen wiper flapping back and forth.

There are no sharp coordinates: I have no photos of the house where Brian lived till he was seven. But Eric, standing in its approximate location, conjures it in his mind: four rooms; a verandah out the front with steps, at the foot of which the dog died after it ate fox bait. Tom and Doris's bedroom, front right; a sitting room, front left, where wedding presents lay undisturbed on a black sideboard, easy chairs too good to sit in. The kitchen on one side at the back, with a white-lace-curtained window looking down across the paddocks, the woodfire stove, the table upon which Doris worked to prepare food and, running along the side of the table, a long stool on which two or three little boys could perch. The other back room, where the boys slept.

Eric's memories come to him as miniatures as he stands and listens and looks around the hillside. By the back door there was a box on which sat an enamel basin where his father washed up after working. He sees his father's dark-haired arms, the black black hairs amid the white white froth of the Lifebuoy soap, the big red cake of Lifebuoy soap. And he sees his father out in the paddock one day — just over there, he points, *right there*, as if he has this minute discovered him and I will see him, too, if I look (but I see only a featureless wave of yellow windblown grass). He sees his father with the grey draught horse Billy yoked and harnessed to a heavy log: Tom making the horse drag the log around the gravel hilltop, teaching it to do what *he* wanted, not what *it* wanted.

At that precise moment on the hillside, in the wind of the afternoon, Eric realises that he cannot clearly picture his father's face as he saw him as a child. He can better see their neighbour, Mr Downie. He can form a clear vision in his mind of Mr Downie, his golf-ball-sized carbuncle bulging on his hand; but the image of his own father's face escapes him, he tells me.

His mother? Well, yes, of course he can see her in his memory easily enough, since she was always around, warm and comforting; but Tom remains a shadow. On the farm, he was always off working, and afterwards he was away so much, sand-carting, log-hauling, or shearing. Eric stands a moment longer, looking across the valley. 'Hmm,' he says, with a little smile to wrap away the sentiment, and turns towards the car.

A STORY TOLD about Tom and Brian: Miss Henry — who was the teacher at the one-room, one-teacher Kirk's Rock school attended by Brian and Eric, the school once sited at the base of the hill below the house — Miss Henry boarded on a farm on the other side of their property, and would walk past every morning on her way to school. (So it would have been she who found them in the event of any throat-slitting.) One day, at school, the story goes, Miss Henry said to Brian, 'Was that your father I saw ploughing today, Brian?'

And he said, 'Was he swearing, Miss Henry?'

And she said, 'No.'

And he said, 'Then it wasn't my father.'

There were only a dozen children in the whole school, from three or four families in the district, and after those kids grew up or moved away there was no one else to be taught. So, one day just before the war, some men came and lifted the schoolhouse onto a truck and drove it away in search of students elsewhere.

Much later, the shire council or the local Rotary club (their members were the same) erected, in the spirit of the historical boards going up in town, a little metal plaque on a brick plinth to mark what had formerly existed on that patch of earth below Kirk's Rock. The plinth stands by itself, unannounced, in the middle of a small paddock. Some roof iron, maybe from the old school dunny, rusts under a nearby tree.

Eric and I step over the wire fence of the paddock and walk across to get a closer view of the plinth. It is brutally nondescript, a forlorn stake driven into the ground of history.

At NIGHT, the wind sighed in the she-oaks. Rabbits crowded up against the fence around the backyard, clamouring to get in. In the morning, walking across the paddock, you could see the sunlight sparkling on little droplets of dew caught on the wide leaves of sundews.

When Tom and Gordon Downie helped each other out, fixing up a machine or putting in a shed, it was Brian or Eric's job to take the *morning lunch* out to the fields: a big enamel billy of tea, a bottle filled with milk, and fresh scones or sandwiches wrapped in a tea towel. The rest of the time it'd be Tom out there on his own, cursing, feeding and harnessing his eight draught horses, chaining them up to the plough or header.

Nobody visited or was invited. The house was too small, and the whitewashed hessian walls nothing to be proud of, after all. Instead, for entertainment, they would ride Florence over for an evening at the Downies', where the adults played bridge and the kids were put to bed on the verandah.

The Downies' house was bigger, with solid mudbrick walls and cool concrete floors covered in kangaroo-skin rugs. The kitchen, Eric told me, smelt of kerosene fridge and apples. The apples came on the train in cases sent by their friends, the Petronis, down in Donnybrook.

Mrs Downie would greet Brian and Eric with a loaf of freshly baked bread under one arm and a knife in the other, and ask them what they wanted on their bread. 'Dripping,' would come their reply, and she would slap a thick coat of dripping on the end of the loaf before sawing through it with her knife, holding the slice from falling with her thumb as she got near the other side, and handing it to each of them atop the blade. The entire feat accomplished in mid-air, as it were.

Leaving the Downies', Tom would carry the boys out to Florence, lay them down on a mattress on the tray, and tuck a blanket over them. It is not hard to imagine, on the journey home, Brian and Eric gazing up into the night sky and watching the patterns of the passing salmon gums illuminated in the headlights. They knew the soothing, familiar rhythm of the gates, and how many there were to stop at, open, go through, stop again, close, and leave behind. They knew the sounds of Florence idling, their father's boots, the tinkling of the latch, the hinges squeaking, and the silent clouds against the moon.

DID I MENTION THE RABBITS? Eric says, 'You have no idea what rabbits were like then, they were thick as fleas. You'd come over a hillside and the hill would look as though it was moving, there were so many rabbits.' It seemed that everybody in the country was busy catching rabbits in those days; even the train drivers on the branch-line Mixed Goods services would stop their trains in the middle of nowhere and leap out to check their traps.

Brian and Eric employed their holidays from high school in trapping rabbits at the farm of their uncle Jack, Doris's brother-in-law, down at Wagin. Each morning, the two boys ventured out early to check the traps they had set where the warren-holes appeared above the creek bank. In the May holidays, the rabbits only wore their light summer pelts, so you might need 12 to weigh a pound, but by August the thick winter pelts had grown. These brought twice the bounty. The boys approached each snared rabbit, banged it on the head with a stick, and slung it on another stick to carry home across their shoulders. At the shed, they skinned them, peeling the skin off each rabbit's back like a wetsuit. They hung the stack of skins in a row to dry, then packed them up in bundles to be ferried on the back of Uncle Jack's ute to the local stock and station agents, Elders, where sometimes the price was good and sometimes it wasn't. Whatever the sum amounted to, it became the pocket money that they took home to Perth at the end of the holidays on the train. And their pockets never felt so strong and heavy.

ALL THIS I KNOW because of Eric telling me stories, driving in his car and at his home in its strange, cartoon-clean suburb in Perth. He is a reliable witness; his memories, I have faith in.

Uncle Noel, on the other hand, chiming in from the back seat — or anywhere, for that matter — is *unreliable*. There is something about the way he talks. Each and every anecdote, as he launches it into the air, begins to sound increasingly implausible, as if the arithmetic is wrong, the geometry askew. He's always had this trouble in the family: nobody quite buying anything he says. I want to believe his stories, but every time he starts I can feel my eyebrows narrowing — and Eric's, too.

Eric, driving, doesn't say anything. You don't want to encourage Noel. Once he gets started, it can be an avalanche of cranky supposition.

I need to stop for a moment and tell you about Uncle Noel. If Brian, and his death, was the hidden mystery in the family, Noel was the mystery staring us in the face at every family gathering: every Sunday night at Gran's, to start with.

Noel lived with Gran in a sleep-out at the back. He had a small dog that he loved called Ned, a bitzer, white with black splotches. Noel had always lived with Gran, it seemed. Never married, never had a girlfriend (or a boyfriend). There was something wrong with Noel, but what that something was remained unclear.

He was an alcoholic, to start with. At 13, being unusually tall, he told me, as if this matter of his height explained it, he started drinking at the Royal Hotel in the city. The Royal was right beside the bus stop home from Perth Boys' School. He was given two bob for lunch each day but, he said, 'I didn't like the lunches, so I'd have three glasses of beer on the way home.' He went on: 'I was 13, and it was 21 drinking age. I got the extra coupons during the war for being overweight and over-height.' The combination of being tall and able to go to pubs was his special attribute as a teenager, since he excelled neither at school, like Brian and Eric, nor on the sports field, like younger brother Andrew.

Many of his stories of himself revolved around alcohol. He told me: 'In '51, the Australian Surf Championships were held at Scarborough, and I was the social secretary of the surf club, and the publican got the idea that I was a good lad — gave me the keys to the cellar. And we had a barbeque that started on the Easter Monday and finished on the Friday morning. I'd go home and have a shower, and go back. After that, Dad gave me a couple of lectures about alcoholism and all this watch-it. He told me to watch out not to get into the grip of grog, and I almost said: "like you".'

And how he first met my mother's parents, soon after she married Brian. Brian, who was up in the bush, had asked Noel to see his parents-in-law, Jack and Barbara, off at Fremantle. They were travelling to Europe on a cargo ship of the Hamburg-American Line that carried about ten passengers.

He told me: 'I was down in their cabin, and next thing the captain walks in and says, "Gee, this is a dry send-off," and next thing the beer starts arriving. I was on my own, never met them before. It was getting quite convivial, and then I happened to notice that I wasn't quite steady on my feet. The captain had departed, and other officers had joined us, and I didn't quite know what was going on. I had to be brought back from Gauge Roads: the ship had sailed. I was still on it.'

The ship had sailed without them telling him. And he had had a few too many. It was the story of his life.

In the year before Noel died, I spoke to him, in his housing-commission flat in Perth's inner north, about Brian and the family. I perched, in the dark afternoon, amid the mess. He said, in his eyes-wide, swear-on-the-Bible manner, that Brian 'was the best brother that anyone could have had'.

He said, 'Nobody was more shocked than I to hear about his first attempt; nobody explained.' He said, 'I actually took the phone call informing us about Brian [when he died]. I had to contact everyone, subsequently — and the story is, from certain sides of the family, that I can't handle things!'

He looked at me, amazed, and reiterated, in case I'd missed the import: 'I answered the phone at Abbott Street from the police.'

'Years later,' he went on, 'I used to take a cup of tea in to Mum in the morning, and a plate of All Bran and stuff, and I took a plate in and she'd died, and I had to contact everyone about that.' He shook his head slowly. 'It's strange. All through, more or less, I've handled everything. They still say I'm the weak link or whatever — can you work it out? I can't. But, as I said earlier, he was one terrific brother.'

He went to take a piss, which he said he had to do sitting

down for certain reasons. I noticed a pile of X-rated videos near the telly.

'I reckon it's a blot on everything that he didn't live, because he would have revolutionised farming Australia-wide,' Noel started up again, his eyes agleam. 'I reckon, if Brian had survived, Australia now would be the food bowl of the world. If he'd received the treatment. But at that stage, it was like a lot of things; they were just as much in the dark as we were.'

This line of thought led on effortlessly, by way of a psychiatrist Brian and Noel had both known, called Michael Clarke, to the time Noel 'did a bit of stupidity, thinking I was a crusader', and tried to blackmail a bloke from down the road who had hit-and-run a young American motorcyclist into hospital. I went with the flow.

'I finished up getting pulled in by the cops,' said Noel, 'so Michael Clarke got me committed to Heathcote for a week for psychiatric assessment.' If there is shame in this, he doesn't show it.

'Glorious time. I was helping everyone there, even went and gathered banana fronds for an evening they were having there for the patients.' He grins. 'It was like rest camp, really.'

I think the story's over, but it's not. He leans forward, his eyes piercing. 'The cop called in, made sure Mum wasn't home; he said, "We're not taking it any further, we're dropping the case; but don't do anything like that again, we've marked your file and everything." Then he proceeded to — see, the bloke that did it had a Golden Fleece service station, a fleet of taxi trucks; he finished up with nothing. This cop bled him of about $400,000. But, of course, who was blamed? The fellow found out that I was involved, somehow, and tried to have a go at me at the Nookenburra Hotel one evening. They straightened him out.'

You see what I mean about his stories? Which bits are true? Are they all true? Then why, for many years, did he catch the bus up the hill every day from Gran's to work at a used-car yard that no longer employed him? And was it true that he later had a car accident that put him on sickness benefits? That he was suing for big damages, but getting done-over by the *bloody courts*? That a strange bone was growing in his cheek in the wake of the accident?

I never asked him about these things; I am not a good reporter. But, in the end, with my video camera rolling and the sun fading on the brick wall out the window, he told me his greatest secret: the sex one. In his childhood, he had an operation that went terribly wrong. An operation on his balls. They cut something by mistake. It meant he could never have sex, never achieve an erection. He had to piss sitting down.

This explained everything (even the X-rated videos?). This would fuck you up.

I asked Eric about it afterwards, as he drove me home in his car on the road past Bold Park. Did he know about this awful secret? Did such an operation, with its sweeping consequences, occur? But, as usual, neither Eric nor anyone else could positively corroborate Noel's story.

Brian shot himself, Andrew impaled his head on a fence as a child and nearly died, Eric bore the family on his back, but Noel was the unlucky brother.

છ૭

Meanwhile, in 1934, back at Kirk's Rock, Eric had joined Brian in the schoolroom with Miss Henry to prance along after the dot-dot-dash of the explorers.

Doris was busy in the hessian house on the hill with her fourth baby, Andrew, and the toddler, Noel. But poor Tom: out in the yards, all Tom's hard work was blowing away in the dust of the Great Depression. Tom had neither the capital nor the experience to ever enjoy a comfortable footing on the farm. Perhaps he would have gained them given time; but the world conspired against him. Far away, the stock markets imploded, wheat and wool prices fell like hail. The bank's head office was cutting its losses, and the local manager at Wickepin had to look after his own kids first.

The humiliation of the bills that she couldn't pay weighed Doris down, scurrying up Yealering's main street, begging credit at the shops. To be reduced to this was bad enough — but out here, closer to the desert than the city? As she was later heard more than once to say, she could not bear the prospect of her sons growing up barefoot *country bumpkins*.

Downing beers at the Commercial, Tom watched his dreams of landed style and grace slither to the shithouse.

I have a friend whose father also grew up in the Depression. After the father's death, they found cupboards stacked high with paper and plastic bags, jam jars, and containers. Nothing was thrown out. And my mother: she knows how to pick every last scrap off a chop or chicken bone. She finds a meal in what her children and grandchildren carelessly leave behind.

Chapter Six

Brian and his family arrived in, what was for him, the fabulous metropolis of Perth sometime in 1934. Trams and trains and trucks weaved in and out and underneath each other in a brilliant, clanging mass of metal and hot-tar roads. Impossibly tall and proper ladies and gents raced along the windblown footpaths. Sailing boats and ferries criss-crossed a river wider than the lake back home, a river that stayed wet all year round. Huge shop windows displayed every possible temptation.

And the ocean! A train ride away lay fabled Cottesloe Beach, where even Brian's anxious mother relaxed under the pine trees. All the city kids were fish, diving under the waves as if native there. The sliding water gave the sand a crust of coolness, made for sinking toes in, building canals and moats and forts in. When the sea breeze arrived, chopping up the ocean and making the sand sting on his back, Brian could wrap up with a towel and, if Doris's father, Grandpa Lorimer, was providing, enjoy the greatest treat of all: an ice cream.

The new school that the boys enrolled in at North Perth had an abundance of teachers and a multitude of rooms. You could get lost there in the corridors and alleys. Only kids of the same age sat in classes together. Everyone wore shoes to school, except for those who, it was whispered, *couldn't afford them*. Doris made sure that Brian and Eric were not suspected of the latter.

Brian, at the age of nine, shouldered the responsibility as the eldest brother to walk Noel up the hill for his first day at school. Doris had decided that she needed to stay home with Andrew, and Tom was away working. Brian held Noel's hand and coaxed him from his fears. 'There is nothing to worry about,' he said as they walked along, 'The teacher won't do anything bad to you.' Noel, buoyed by the confidence of his big brother, managed to cross the threshold into his classroom without so much as a single blubber. He treasured this triumphant moment as his first memory of Brian.

Tom, watching shabby dole queues stretch along the streets, was forced to travel to put food on the table for the family. He had knocked on the door at Elders, where he still knew a few blokes whom he thought he could trust; but they couldn't take on anybody, so they said, not with business the way it was. He headed back to the Murchison and set up as a shearing contractor, dragging a gang of shearers from station to station on an old Bedford truck.

Doris remained behind in Perth with the four children,

surviving on the money that Tom sent down. The house that they rented had a big lilac tree in the backyard with a rope swing tied to it on which Brian stretched back, gazed into the fathomless, deep-blue Perth sky, and imagined he was flying.

Once a week, Doris took the boys on the bus trip to South Guildford to do her mother's washing, changing buses in the city on the way.

The house of Brian's Grandma and Grandpa Lorimer was recognisable by its smelly hedge and the washed gravel path from which his grandma continually swept leaves.

Brian's youngest brother, Andrew, has memories of this time and place that come to him as scents and fragrances. Inside Grandma's kitchen: the sweet, nutty aroma of caraway seeds baked in biscuits, which 'you would have for morning tea or any time you could talk her into giving you one'. Outside, in season: the ripe odour of loquats, peaches, and nectarines on the trees; fat grapes dripping from the vine, begging to be scoffed. Grandpa in his workshop: fresh pine-shavings curling, moist, from the tongue of his plane in the making of a beautiful wooden box that would afterwards be painted white. This white box, with its secret drawer in the bottom, disguised in the pattern of the framework, a little finger-shaped indentation to slide it open; the precious *white box* that Andrew would inherit after Grandpa died, and fill its secret drawer with his collection of deadly shanghais.

Andrew, six years' Brian's junior, is the iron man of the family — the strapping, later grizzled surfing bloke. Framed in his study is a photo of himself and his two adult sons, taken on a beach. They are standing side by side on the sand, naked, with their bum-cheeks towards the camera, the crashing waves beyond. Each of their torsos forms a cartoon Mr Universe triangle, shoulders wide as doorways. Andrew's jaw, if he turned to face us, would be locked square, his mouth a sideways crinkle emitting dry remarks from one corner or the other. His eyes, we would see, are slits, from a lifetime of squinting into the sun for the next wave.

As a child, wherever possible, Andrew lived entirely outside, emerging from the backyard, the lane, or nearby bush only to stock up on food and sleep. He could pick up any sport and master it. Apart from surfing, he favoured football and swimming. In later life, he became a real estate agent, with the consequence that his early memories (not olfactory) are reviewed through those professional eyes. The Mount Hawthorn home they lived in, he tells me, squinting, was a typical house of that era 'in terms of basic construction'; similar, in fact, if he thinks about it, to their later Wembley house which, on the east side of the street facing west, was 'a typical house built prior to the war'. As he thinks about them, he can't help but calculate the appreciation in their property value since those times.

Can he remember anything else about the Mount Hawthorn house? He shifts his jaw back and forth. 'There was a pretty good swing in the backyard,' he says, finally, raising an eyebrow as he momentarily re-enters the world-view of the feral child. This was the swing attached to the tree from which Andrew fell at the age of ten to impale his head upon the picket fence. Doris hurried him to the hospital with the picket still stuck in his skull.

'Yeah,' says Andrew, and grins, 'Yeah, that was a ... yeah,

that wasn't too good,' with the well-honed Australian art of understatement that probably helped him sound convincing at open-house inspections.

∽

A couple of years went by, and still Tom found no work in the city. With the threads of the family unravelling over the distances between them, Tom heard, in 1937, of an opportunity log-hauling for a timber mill in Mandurah, a small town on an estuary south of Perth. It was close enough that he could persuade Doris to move their whole family down to reunite.

Brian was ten and Eric eight. Old enough to roam by the river any time school was out. One time, I hear, Brian made a telephone in the sand dunes with tin cans and some string. It is a flimsy memory of Eric's that I grab and nurture. I can imagine myself being there: barefoot, watching. Brian instructs Eric to wait on top of a sandhill, holding one tin can, while he marches to the top of the next sandhill, carrying the other. The string stretches across between them, and they try to pull it tight. Brian is inspired by a book that he's read, called *Things To Do for Boys*. He talks into his can, and Eric, cupping his can to his ear, can hear every word — although, whether through the wire or the air, he can't quite be sure. But Brian tells him it is a good telephone.

Another time in Mandurah, Brian and Eric were playing in the river. Eric made a discovery. I am tempted to co-opt this discovery for Brian, as my protagonist, but I feel I mustn't; the experience is so clear and vivid in Eric's mind that it would be unfair to dislodge it. Doris was fishing for poddy whiting in the clear water behind the Peninsula Hotel, catching them by the bucketload on the sandy bottom there, with a simple hook-and-sinker line that she'd rigged. Eric, nearby in the shallows on his hands and knees, put his face under the water to examine the riverbed.

This opening of eyes under water was in itself a revelation, as I can attest. As a young child, I never for many years dared try such a thing, since I believed that eyes were insubstantial objects, not unlike raw egg-yolks floating in their whites, and that, if I opened my eyes underwater, nothing would stop the liquid flowing in at their corners and flooding the inside of my body. Later, I accepted this idea to be false, and perhaps liable to ridicule, but I defended the logic of my earlier belief by comparing it with other facts no less fanciful but true, such as that a bee must die as soon as it has stung you.

But I digress. Eric was underwater, looking at the bottom, and this was his discovery: stretched out, his legs bobbed behind him; and, if he raised his hands, too, off the sandy riverbed, he didn't sink! His whole body floated. Suspended, hovering, as if by magic. Meanwhile, the riverbed was slowly sliding by beneath him, so it must be he flowing the other way with the current.

This is how Eric learnt to swim. In those days, there were no lessons, just as there were none earlier, when Frederick Cecil taught Uncle Ben to swim by throwing him off the Rockingham Jetty.

In 1938, the timber mill in Mandurah went broke. Tom was given notice, the family forced to pack up and move again. The boys disappeared from another school.

This time, they landed up for several months on Rottnest Island, where Tom employed his truck to cart sand and materials for military construction. The smell of war was in the air. Twelve miles off the coast of Perth, Rottnest, later synonymous with summer beach holidays and previously an Aboriginal prison, at this time guarded the port of Fremantle as a strategic-defensive position. Tom helped build gun emplacements in the sand dunes and on the limestone promontories.

The Carlins lived in a small, wooden bungalow encased on all sides with lattice walls — perhaps even the same house that we rented on holidays in the seventies. A row or two of these antique bungalows, 100 metres back from the beach at Thomson Bay, are now redolent with nostalgic charm and the salt and peppermint smell of countless carefree childhoods. Sad-eyed quokkas still hover nearby like methadone survivors, bleary-eyed and pockmarked. Bicycles sail past merrily, ferrying snorkellers and afternoon expeditioners. The ghosts of Brian and his brothers amble in the shadows.

Only so many gun emplacements could plausibly be installed on Rottnest; once they were completed, Tom was yet again unemployed. With precious few options, Tom and Doris temporarily split the family to seek refuge with their own parents. Doris and the two small ones stayed at fragrant South Guildford with the Lorimers; Tom, Brian, and Eric joined the dour household of old Frederick Cecil and Auntie Jess in Blencowe Street, West Leederville.

For a proud man who had once fancied his prospects, the

son of a distinguished figure in the community from a line of solid bourgeois, Tom must have felt he had reached rock bottom: unable to provide under his own roof for his family. The wordless dinners at his father's table, his little sister serving up their food, and his two young sons watching him across the table must have been just about unbearable.

Even Jess, a *woman*, had retained all this time her position with Brown & Dureau in the city. I imagine her there in the mornings, dolled up in her latest outfit, swinging out the door to catch the trolley bus. I imagine Frederick Cecil, too, enacting the well-worn daily rituals of an unfaltering career: straightening his tie in the hallway mirror, clicking the front gate shut, and striding off for his large office — where, no doubt, his secretary *Miss Whatsaname* would be answering the phone and ready to take dictation — with its splendid oak desk and leather chair, its framed citations and photographs, its window that Frederick might slide open to receive the breeze with his afternoon Wedgwood tea and biscuit.

Then, I imagine Tom, sprucing himself up as best he could six days a week and searching for an opening, his truck no longer wanted anywhere; finally, I'm told, reduced to labouring on concrete slabs for a pipe company.

But those gun emplacements had Tom thinking, I reckon. He had liked the smell of those things, their well-oiled sleekness; and he had liked the smart tilt of the officers who came to inspect them, their shiny new shoes and uniforms, their camaraderie in the mess tent. The puff of their chests. These blokes had a mission, a team; they had respect. They weren't shit-kicking around like any old no-hoper, scrounging to put bread in front of their kids. Tom decided to join the militia.

The militia, the volunteer Army Reserve of that time, operated weekend training exercises and annual camps. He signed up with the local brigade, and immediately felt at home. He liked the marching, the rigour, the discipline — and the beers afterwards. He walked down the street with a new vision of himself. He was part of something bigger, something important, even noble. Who knew what would be happening with Hitler? Or the Russians, for that matter? More than enough people saw dark clouds coming.

Things at last started looking up, Eric told me. Tom saved enough money to rent a house in West Leederville, near Brian and Eric's primary school. They all moved back in together. Tom got a new job, requiring a suit and tie and the application of his intellect rather than his back and shoulders: selling insurance. Not ideal, but a step up.

I imagine there were people in the army that took a shine to him. His commanding officers in the militia saw that he had potential. Before too long, there were conversations over drinks along the lines of making a career of this whole army caper: the forces were always on the lookout for bright young talent. If he was no longer young at 37, it was not too late — he should at least consider it. He was flattered. They shouted him a beer. They clinked glasses. He went home and told Doris what he had decided.

Doris wondered how the pay compared with what he brought home currently. She thought about the house with proper walls that she'd like to buy, and the little extras here and there: new shoes, toys, that nice tablecloth she'd seen at Boans department store in the city. She wondered where the army would send him, and whether he'd be at home with the family any more than before. Whether there'd be a war, and he'd be sent off fighting and end up crippled. Or dead. Whether — she knew it was wrong, though who could help but think about it in passing — she'd be able to manage on the widow's pension.

Tom signed all the necessary papers and gave notice at the insurance firm. Suddenly, the treads of a future opened up ahead: it wasn't going to be too hard for a man like him to make his mark in the forces, work his way up the ladder. He took pleasure in the shining of his shoes. The discipline, the hardness, the sheer *masculinity* of it all — he found it changed his breathing, made him taller. Doris noticed, for a time, a newfound insistence in the bedroom. He told the blokes at the pub what he was up to, and watched their eyes in their beers, as they measured their own courage.

But he remained distant from his sons, Eric told me. They encountered him if not across the silent dinner table then at the other end of the razor strop. Discipline and punishment of these children played out in a cruel and protracted ritual, albeit one perhaps not uncommon in its day.

First would come the misdemeanour: Brian or one of his brothers crossing a line, behaving badly. Doris was witness and prosecutor, and sometimes victim, too, in one way or another; she battled at the front line of the children's behaviour, where Tom, invariably, was absent. But Doris never meted out punishment for crimes committed by the boys; her role was merely to proclaim the fateful injunction: 'Wait till your father gets home!'

Tom's schedule determined the appointed hour, which might be later the same day, or a week or a month afterwards. Doris reported the summary of offences, and Tom, the dutiful executioner, trudged off to the bathroom for the strop. For the sentenced child: the humiliation of pants dropped to the ankles, the pain of lashings on tender flesh. Meanwhile, Doris fled to the bedroom and hid her head under the pillow to smother the anguished cries of her poor baby.

Looking back now from old age, Eric feels sorry for Tom: the Tom trapped in this paternal duty, forcing himself to enact this violent sentence upon his children for crimes he knows only via hearsay. But Brian, as a young man, grew to hate his father for his cold cruelty. I was told that once, as a teenager, seeing Tom fetching the strop to wallop Noel, Brian summoned all his courage to confront his father at the bathroom door. 'You shouldn't hit him, you don't even know what happened!' Brian, the eldest son, feeling keenly the responsibility of his position: it must be he, if anyone, to resist the tyrant. But Tom just snarled and brushed him aside, and Brian saw himself forever after weak and pathetic in his father's eyes.

Brian was not naturally a fighter. He preferred words to fists, his tongue sharper and stronger than his lightly framed body. But he had to learn where and when his weapons of sarcasm and mockery might get him into trouble. Just about the first day at West Leederville Primary, Eric said, Dicky Millett flattened Brian with a left hook to stop him mimicking Dicky's hare-lipped way of speaking.

And out on the tip at West Leederville, collecting bamboo sticks one time, Eric said, he and Brian ran into the José kids from over the road. The Carlin boys were taught to look down on the Josés — they were common and trashy (you didn't need to say the word 'wog'), and their house smelt. Eric had already been caught illicitly associating with Colin José, lured against his better judgment by Colin's unparalleled collection of Phantom comics. Tom had laid down the law at dinner: 'You WILL NOT play with that boy.' Now, at the tip, Brian thought to demonstrate the superiority of the Carlins over the Josés with one or two wittily snide remarks tossed in their direction. Tony José stepped straight up and — *smack!* — gave him one, as they said in the comics, right on the jaw. Brian fell over and backed away, retreating, as always, from physical conflict.

'I should have stood up for him more that day,' said Eric, even though he was the younger brother.

Chapter Seven

Listen, in 1942: first, the drone. A low hum vibrating across the red-brick tiles and chimneys of the Perth suburbs, rising inexorably until it seems to fill the air with expectation.

A plane appears, grinding a path through the sky, heavy and low — the very plane that Brian has glued together piece by piece, in miniature, in his bedroom. Now comes another and another, and soon they encompass the horizons, a hive of identical metal insects powering steadily southwards in unison, as if joined ingeniously with invisible rods or magnets of some kind. It is the mighty Americans arriving at last. The squadrons of Super Flying Fortresses wallpapering the air are patterned with smaller cousins, two-engined Boeings.

Afterwards comes an even more remarkable species, with giant paws stretched out beneath, looming so close it seems, if

Brian were on the roof, that he could reach out and touch them: these are the fabled Catalina Flying Boats that they say can fly without stopping for ten hours on end, land on water, and float — although you would think that their vast bulk should sink them, plop, like skimming stones coming to rest.

Now the thrill of the war has really come to Perth. Before this, it had been sombre notes on the radio in the voices of Mr Churchill and Mr Curtin, to which the adults listened with grave attention. It had been delicious maps in the newspapers of exotic far-off places with snaking arrows marking the flow of armies: our boys and the Hun; at school, the Geography teacher hammering on the cracking map of Europe with his pointer. And Movietone serials with ominous chords and headlines bursting from the screen: *Hitler marches into Paris! The Blitz hits London!*

But now the Japs are involved, and the Yanks, and Perth is an Important Base of Operations. The streets are filled with soldiers and sailors coming and going en route to theatres in Asia and the Middle East.

Households make ready with blackout curtains and ration cards. Those who have the money build concrete bomb-shelters in their backyards.

The Yanks are suddenly everywhere: at the beach, on the trolley buses, spilling out of pubs. Bigger than normal people, they grin with impossible charm. Brian watches them helping young mothers with their prams and skipping down footpaths, which *they* don't call footpaths. They are putting on a show, with the whole town as their audience.

Other Yanks shun the limelight, the quiet ones you would see clinging to the straps on buses, looking lost. They gaze anxiously down passing streets, as if searching for a familiar landmark, or expecting to see a friend from home. And the Negroes: black as the ace of spades, as Grandma Lorimer might have put it, deep chocolate-brown skin that Brian has never seen outside a movie or a book. Who knows how *they* talk?

They're rich, the Yanks; they splash money like there's no tomorrow. People say they do a lot of drinking, which makes them even louder, bigger, grinning-er. You want to stay out of their way in Barrack Street or Freo come nine o'clock, when the pubs shut down the beer taps and push them out the doors.

All the girls at Perth Modern School are mad about them, just like their older sisters — every girl in town, it looks to be. Brian overhears the older generation muttering about it over shop counters, nudging each other on buses: look at her *all dolled up* with her arm slunk round one of *them*. The Aussie blokes have gone off to defend the Empire in Singapore and New Guinea and the Middle East, and left behind an awful lot of young wives and girlfriends, and other females too young or wallflowery to be wives and girlfriends yet, and the Yanks are getting fresh with all of them.

What's he promised her? My Brian hears them whisper. *Where are they off to? She got some local boy away fighting somewhere while this Yank's here with his wallet hanging open and his tongue hanging out?* He watches the pursing of the lips and the knotting of the brows. One invasion protecting them against another invasion, so they told each other: *Not that the other one wouldn't be worse, of course. At least the Americans are, well, more like us. But — well, sometimes you wonder.*

Eric told me there were always big fights between the Yank sailors, the Aussies, and the Kiwis. One time, he said, he remembers being in Murray Street in the city, and seeing a mass of drunken Kiwis on the verandah of the Australia Hotel, next door to the Boans emporium. A couple of the Kiwis had unscrewed the giant glass spheres from the light fittings on the roof of the verandah, and were holding them aloft above the street. 'Charlie, I'll just drop it down to you', promised one of them, and let his sphere tumble through the air to an almighty *smash!* on the pavement, cue to a cacophony of cheers, whistles, and curses, as people fled its path.

Further down the street, Eric saw more drunken Kiwis carry a couple of 'baby' Austin 7 motor cars, which they had found parked nearby, up the stairs and through the front door of the post office in Forrest Place, where they deposited them, for a laugh, in the middle of the postal hall. For a teenage boy, it was a thrilling carnival of danger and revelry.

જ્જ

During the war, Brian attended high school: Perth Modern School, the government's showcase for the state's most promising, which selected only 50 girls and 50 boys each year on academic merit. Future prime minister Bob Hawke would be in the class two years behind Brian, and Rolf Harris, renowned at the time as a champion swimmer, another year below.

When Brian won his place at the Modern School, Tom and Doris bought for him a splendid brand-new school blazer. Eric remembers Brian standing in their kitchen at West Leederville trying on the blazer, and himself bursting into tears, knowing family finances would never stretch to buying *him* a blazer, when and if his own time came to win a place at the school (on which point he was proved right, he adds as a footnote).

I picture Brian modelling the blazer for the family. He slips it over his shoulders and notices in the mirror how wide and strong he looks in it. He can imagine himself becoming a man.

When I look for Brian at that age, brushing puberty, I find instead, not for the first time, my own reflection. My earliest adolescent sexual experiments were conducted in secret either by myself or with a friend who lived a few streets away, as we curiously compared stiffies. I had developed an interest in photography at that time, setting up my own darkroom in our outside dunny by placing the enlarger on a makeshift bench perched above the toilet bowl. I took photos of my friend, and another boy I knew, lying naked in a stream in a national park that we visited on a picnic, and developed them myself in my darkroom. I didn't think about it in a sexual way but, nevertheless, took precautions to store my prints discreetly. And I didn't think it important to show my models how pretty they looked, lolling in the water. Even when my friend and I, on a sleepover one night, went so far as to contemplate the experiment of anal intercourse with each other, it was only, we firmly believed, in the interest of researching how the real thing with girls might feel. We attempted it briefly, without conviction, coming to the definitive conclusion that it was physically impossible to achieve any penetration of that orifice.

Our outward sexual focus remained on girls, but they were, unfortunately, an impossibly distant species that could only be discussed in abstract terms. We knew about the four stages of sexual conquest, each a higher base-camp en route to Everest. We knew that, as would have been self-evident to teenage boys the world over, this was the single path and the single destination:

Stage one: kissing. We'd done that already in Grade Six, under the stage of the primary school hall and sometimes on the floor at Grade Six parties. That was no big deal (although how the tongue should be appropriately employed was still a question).

Stage two: the approach to the breasts, coming either down from the shoulders or up from the waist, and being allowed to touch them under jumpers and suchlike.

Stage three: the green light to venture with fingers *down there*, to that most mysterious zone inside the panties with the pubes.

Stage four: needless to say, the final assault on the summit — *doing it*. We all knew what that was, although how it worked in the field was another matter. Each of these stages, it was believed, was best achieved by stealth, picking one's way forward further and further into uncharted territory, moving so subtly as to slip undetected past enemy checkpoints.

When, a few years later at age 15, I was finally able to start putting my theories into practice in the company of a real-live girl, I was astonished — and thrilled — to discover how *keen* she was about the whole thing.

'Have you ever done this before?' she asked as we kissed on her brother's vinyl beanbag to Blondie's 'Heart of Glass'.

'Yes,' I said. I had to lie. She already had a proper boyfriend with a car. I had a lot of ground to make up.

I believe Brian's formal sexual education, like Eric's, arrived in a brown envelope. 'This is for you to read,' I can hear Doris saying, thrusting it at him in the hallway. 'And when you have read it, give it back,' before fleeing to the kitchen and the safety of a mixing bowl.

The letter, from the government, outlined the many horrors of sex in baffling detail. Brian would have read the letter in the privacy of his sleep-out and absorbed the seriousness of its message, if not the confusing technical descriptions of the finer points. But, still, I bet he touched himself and felt bad afterwards.

He made friends among the girls at school, from what Eric said. He liked girls; he didn't have to compete with them. He charmed them with his witty asides and neat, handsome looks. He was a boy whom a girl could one day bring home knowing her parents would be impressed.

ↄ

Early in 1942, amid concerns that young children should be evacuated from Perth in case the Japanese bombers struck — as they did from February onwards in Darwin, Broome, and other places in the north — the *little ones* in the Carlin family, Andrew and Noel, were sent away to the country with Doris for six months. They caught the train back to Yealering, and lodged with their former neighbours, the Downies, at Kirk's Rock.

Tom was away, of course, on deployment with the army, but Brian and Eric remained in Perth, boarding with Grandpa

Frederick Cecil and Auntie Jess in the dark house at Blencowe Street, so that their senior schooling would not be interrupted. With their mother away, the boys apparently found more freedom to roam the city.

Eric got himself a job selling the *Daily News*, tuppence a paper, at the top of London Court just by St Georges Terrace, from where he could watch the world go by. He made a small fortune, enough for the Saturday double-feature matinee each week with some left over to buy long trousers.

Brian didn't sell papers; he took a more patrician approach to life, as if above the realm of casual employment. This is how Eric tells it. Eric leapt from one holiday job to the next, riding the city on an orange bike with a carrier full of parcels for United Motors, or receiving goods in the truck bay at the back of Woolworths. Brian, on the other hand, didn't like getting dirty. He didn't like getting grease on himself. It was as if his status as the eldest brother gave him an exemption from the demands of wage labour. He was free to concentrate his weekends on playing lacrosse and tennis. I wonder, if this is true, how he supported himself monetarily?

My Brian, my possible Brian, here finds himself completely crowded out behind the remembered Brian of his brother. I am not sure I want this Brian, the dandy, at home with his model aeroplanes, books, and personal grooming. I am more attracted to Eric, out there in the streets, rolling up his sleeves and having adventures. But I cannot blame Eric for making himself the hero of his own memories; we all do the same.

BEFORE LONG, with fears of imminent Japanese invasion calmed, Brian's family were reunited once again in Perth, moving to the newer suburb of Wembley, west towards the ocean.

The morning newspaper, the *West Australian*, was much fought over in the Carlin house. Brian and Eric connived to be the first to take possession of each issue, both keen to follow the ongoing saga of vast battles that swept back and forth across strange lands: Rommel in the desert, the Nazis stomping through Kiev and Minsk. Meanwhile, Doris sat up in bed reading the Births, Deaths, and Marriages. Someone she knew was always in one or other of the three, and she liked to keep up with all the comings and the goings.

Another paper, *The Mirror*, only appeared on Saturdays, offering a more salacious brand of news. This, the boys had to buy for themselves, if they wanted it. *The Mirror* specialised in punning headlines, preferably hinging on sexual innuendo. Eric remembers one of the finest: 'Mount St Tit Bit', screamed the story of a wild party in Mount Street, Perth, where an American sailor made a gratuitous assault upon a woman's person. It's not hard to see the appeal of this *outrageous* saucy wordplay to an early teenage-boy's sense of humour. Meanwhile, the inner pages of *The Mirror* promised further instalments in the exploits of the legendary local private detective Alf Sleep, who was forever climbing through bedroom windows to capture potential divorcees *in flagrante*.

As 1944 CAME AROUND, Tom applied for a posting overseas to Guadalcanal. For the first time, he was in genuine danger of getting killed. Although Doris would have fretted more than ever, Tom had become such an absent figure that the boys would have scarcely registered the difference.

Perhaps it was most strongly Brian, entering his final year of school, who felt the pressure to take note of the example set by his father's service. As the year went on and Brian approached his university entrance exams, the childhood idea resurfaced of enlisting in the navy. After all, aged 17, it was the only way to become a serviceman: for the army and the air-force, one had to wait to turn 18 and, who knew, the war might be over before then.

I imagine Brian, in his own eyes, would always fall short of what Tom wanted of him. Despise his father as he might, he nevertheless craved his approval. Joining the navy was his opportunity to prove himself *as a man*, whatever that might mean. Tom would have been pleased; hearing the news of Brian's plans, he would have written back warmly. As soon as the final exam was over, Brian visited the recruiting office to sign the necessary papers. At the front gate, in the gathering gloom of a westerly change, I see Doris waving him off.

Chapter Eight

Brian served in the navy from the beginning of 1945 until early 1947, when the Australian forces of the Second World War were finally officially demobilised.

His naval records reveal that he spent the first six months training at HMAS *Cerberus* on the Mornington Peninsula, and was transferred to HMAS *Penguin* on Sydney Harbour in August. He eventually departed for the Pacific theatre of war in 1946, on a Corvette minesweeper named the HMAS *Cowra*. Obviously, the war itself was by now well over: these were mopping-up operations.

Brian returned to Perth in January 1947 a changed man.

I picture Doris, beneath a broad-brimmed hat, waiting with Noel and Andrew for Brian to disembark from the transport ship at the wharf in Fremantle. She wonders whether she will recognise him. Crowds of excited people wave and shout as each sailor emerges from the ship door and steps down the gangway. Those sailors who expect to be met glance around to locate their loved ones below. Some grin from ear to ear, but most effect an air of worldly nonchalance, as befits their new role as returning veterans and heroes. Every now and then, one appears who seems not to notice the crowds at all. He looks ahead impatiently, eyes narrow, jaw set. This is not his homecoming but merely a transit point along the way, and he moves through the crowds quickly, towards the exit of the terminal, searching for taxi or train.

Doris's eyes aren't so good as they once were, and her heart is in her mouth. It is difficult to see anything above the jostling people. Several times, she glimpses a man who might be Brian. Her nerves are getting the better of her. Was that him on crutches? Was there an injury she hadn't been forewarned about? She relies on Noel and Andrew, with their young eyes.

'Hey, Brian!' The boys jump up and down, waving madly. Brian's childhood face emerges in the visage of a man grown taller and broader in his absence. He sees his mother clutching her purse and beaming at him, teary-eyed, his gangly teenage brothers acting the goat behind her.

Fremantle feels like a sketch, a tentative work-in-progress after the great harbour of Sydney. The wool-store buildings make a low wall for the sky. Brian and his brothers compete over how much each has grown, consider the virtues of Doris's cooking versus the navy's offerings, joke about haircuts and facial hair.

Doris mops her cheeks, restraining herself from clutching Brian again in public. Brian shakes hands and waves goodbye to a few colleagues, each trailing away with their own families: the ex-servicemen look like footballers, young and fresh and vital, towering above their swarming relatives.

Back at the family home in Scarborough, Brian lies down on his old bed and listens to the blood pounding through his head. Familiar flies buzz at the window screens. A kookaburra chortles in the backyard. Already, he feels the need to flee his family, to find some peace and quiet. They know nothing about him now.

Tom would be home soon, on leave from his latest posting. He would shake hands with Brian, with that crushing grip of his, and slap him on the shoulders. He would open a ceremonial longneck and offer Brian a beer, man to man. And he would ask professional military questions about dates, distances, and procedures. He would make the jovially snide remarks about the navy that were obligatory for an army careerist, and welcome some good-humoured return fire.

But Brian will go easy in this field, lest he misjudge and blurt out one of the many hostile comments that swim in his mind from time to time towards his father. Tom would narrow his eyes and size his son up as at inspection, for those tell-tale signs of weakness. Why could his son not be strong enough to parry whatever shit was flung at him?

❧

Brian had done well, if not brilliantly, in his final exams at school. It seemed obvious that he should go to university to attain a profession, especially with the support the government gave ex-servicemen to do so. He chose Agriculture, no doubt because of his bond with rural life, growing out of his early years at Kirk's Rock and maintained through all the school holidays spent with the Downies or at Uncle Jack's farm in Wagin; so he could help others to succeed where his father had not.

The new University of Western Australia campus stretched out along the Swan River foreshore at Crawley. In those days, the university was approximately the size of a large high school — small enough for everyone to know everyone. Mature-age ex-servicemen like Brian lent an air of worldly sophistication to proceedings, so vastly experienced and grown-up were they in the eyes of the squeaky-clean ingénues straight from school.

Agriculture, like Engineering and other technical and scientific pursuits, was an almost-entirely male preserve. But the head of Agriculture, Professor Underwood, was widely known to be a cultured, enlightened type. A world leader in his own field of research, he was often steaming off overseas to address expert gatherings. Somewhere, he got the idea that his Agriculture majors should broaden their education by taking subjects in an unrelated field in second year.

Having survived the compulsory all-Science diet of first year — the conglomerated Physics, Chemistry, Biology, and Geology — for many, the second-year elective came as welcome relief. It was then, when many of his classmates chose English Literature or History and involved themselves with the Dramatic Club, that Brian took up Psychology.

Agriculture and Psychology: these choices represented the

two sides of Brian's nature. Agriculture, practical and worthwhile; an opportunity to establish a decent middle-class career in a field in which intellectual challenges could translate into real differences in people's lives. Agriculture, the daylight face Brian presented to the world, the bright young man on the cusp of life. Psychology, the fears that nagged him in the night; the relentless private circles that his mind would etch, gazing out the bus window on shadowy afternoons. But Psychology, also, the fascinating puzzle of these contradictions, of which he was only too aware.

Through Psychology, Brian entered into an exotic new stratum of undergraduate society. His friends in Agriculture were pretty straightforward blokes, active in the rugby and cricket clubs, their idea of culture intimately connected to drinking beer. But in Psychology dwelt all sorts of odd bods. At the Refectory and on the shady campus lawns, Brian found himself admitted to the ranks of the *intellectual set*. These were extravagant, alluring types, determined to bring the heady sophistication of the Left Bank and Bloomsbury, as gleaned from books and magazines and celluloid, to sleepy Perth.

I colour in the scenes from what I'm told: a young man called John, an ex-Gunner in the Royal Air Force, reclines on the grass by Winthrop Hall, propped up on an elbow and waving a cigarette theatrically. Beside him, his wind-up portable gramophone wafts soaring operatic arias into the balmy late-summer air. Arrayed on either side, a dozen men and women swig Brandivino, blowing smoke-rings, philosophising.

The women look as if they might grab your balls before they

kiss you; the men may or not be equally as interested. All the boundaries are fabulously blurred, society's *archaic* conventions transgressed. Some of the women don't even wear bras all the time!

The intellectual set love Sigmund Freud, George Orwell, Jean-Paul Sartre, Arthur Koestler, Joyce. *Ulysses* has escaped the censor's ban in Western Australia, perhaps owing to the state's distance from the orbit of Melbourne's stern Archbishop Mannix, and everyone is reading it, planning to, or pretending to. A screening of Cocteau's *La Belle et la Bête*, one night only at the French Club, must not be missed! Does existentialism explain the melancholia of the world? Is communism significantly different from socialism, and does either offer the new way forward for man, as they claim? On free afternoons, they install themselves at one or other pub — the lounge bar at Steve's by the river, or the Captain Stirling on the highway — where, being broke as always, they make a single brandy-lime-and-soda last long enough to thrash out life's big questions.

This is a chapter of Brian's life that I must confess to encouraging wholeheartedly. I like him being suave and bohemian, gazing up at the stars with Puccini in his ears, appreciating the freedom of imagining the world afresh. It reminds me, romantically, of my younger self and friends, skipping across the Perth suburbs, certain that nobody else had ever truly *lived* as free as we were.

At 18, I moved in, for a brief glorious time, to a rambling old house in Gibney Street, Cottesloe, to live with a bunch of art-school students, including my cousin Michael. It is a time forever bathed in the golden glow of the late-afternoon sun sliding up the hill from the Indian Ocean.

The house itself was mildly famous for being previously occupied by the McComb brothers of the Triffids, the legendary Perth band that we used to watch every weekend at The Stoned Crow hippie-bar on the highway into Freo.

The night that I moved in, I met Fred, who lived in the front room surrounded by elegantly grotesque paintings-in-progress on easels. He had just slashed a portrait of his girlfriend with a Stanley knife, she having broken up with him earlier in the day. He invited me to join him in sinking into vast and tatty armchairs in the lounge room, and in consuming, with an air of dignified melancholy, a bottle of vodka.

In the summer, our parties splashed into the vast tumbledown back garden. Ironically whimsical tape loops of Bing Crosby singing 'If You Go Down to the Woods Today' were set up to greet guests coming down the front path — surrealism dancing with Jonathan Richman. In winter, we stoked up the old pot belly in the kitchen and read Lewis Carroll out aloud, or ate curry and kitchari sitting cross-legged around the tabletop Michael had made but never put legs on.

At Gibney Street, I was unemployed — between universities — and pursuing my artistic interests. I scrounged old 16mm film stock and borrowed a Bolex camera to shoot a film set in my house, in which my housemates and another friend, who later committed suicide, played a nuclear family who one day decide to escape their daily rut by heading off into the sunset on their skateboards.

The skateboarding scenes, played to the evocative although stolen accompaniment of a Lou Reed song, were the main part of the movie. Two of the cast were reasonably good skateboarders, and I composed various lyrical, if dangerous, shots hanging out the windows of moving cars, or lying in the middle of the road with the Bolex as they cruised majestically down hilly backstreets, surfing asphalt waves.

Later, at university in Adelaide, I discovered the intellectual thrill of Theory, which at this time was post-structuralism, deconstruction, Lacanian psychoanalysis, and feminism, to name-drop a few headline acts. I became entranced by the big ideas, equal parts revolutionary, poetic, and obscure, of the various stars in the French pantheon, who only became more intriguing if, at the height of their fame, they were struck by tragedy: Roland Barthes run over by a laundry truck in a Paris street, Althusser going mad and murdering his wife.

For Brian, his time encountering Psychology and its intersection with bohemia was not only exciting but also dangerous. Perhaps he was too prone to the influence of its ideas, which began to form feedback loops in his head. This is what his doctors soon told him.

In Brian's day, everyone in Psychology, in Perth at least, was still a Freudian. Freud was less than ten years dead, and the great sweep of challenges to his authority in the field was yet to come, notwithstanding the early schisms with the likes of Jung. Freud focused the mind on the unconscious and sexuality, a tantalising topic of conversation for those inclined to venture there, and particularly for young people whose opportunities to do more than talk were limited. Most of the men had been away to war and knew something of the world of sex, but the women were younger and, in many cases, had no practical experience in the field. This made theoretical speculation all the more enticing.

Brian, I imagine, suddenly found that, for the first time, he could talk about virtually anything he liked. Freud made clear that it was relatively normal to have all those strange thoughts, desires, and anxieties that flew around his head.

In class, his friends told me, they learnt about the latest developments in psychological testing and later, in the refectory, they experimented on themselves. They tried the Rorschach inkblot tests with much hilarity; they carefully completed the Minnesota Multiphasic Personality Inventory (MMPI), the latest groundbreaking clinical tool for psychological assessment, and enthusiastically postulated hypotheses from their results. The MMPI asked a host of questions about behaviour and attitudes. From the answers, a chart could be plotted against indicative psychological tendencies. It was fun, like one of those silly magazine quizzes but with the gravity of science.

Brian scored high on one particular column, the masculine/ feminine register; so did many of the girls and some of the other men. This seemed to reflect the fact that the girls were loud and forthright and the men a little soft. But the 'h' word came up a lot. Was anybody in the group actually *homosexual*? Following Freud, they knew that everyone may have such latent tendencies, but what this might mean in practice was debatable.

I am reminded of stories told by my mother and my aunt Alison, who both started university a little after Brian (and never joined the intellectual set), of discovering a pair of *lesbians* living at the University Hostel. The matron felt the need to take all the new girls aside and warn them what these *lesbians* were up to, especially since she was apparently powerless to stop them — all the rules and regulations were designed only to prevent immoral behaviour of a heterosexual kind. One of the pair of women was, as Alison remembered thinking of it, the *real* lesbian, whereas the other was her pretty *victim*, the naive girl who had somehow fallen into the spider's web, and who, later on, as if to underscore this character portrayal, happily married and had three children. The words *butch* and *femme* were not in anyone's vocabulary then. The new girls from the country had never heard of such a thing as *lesbianism* before, and were in the dark as to what might take place in those girls' narrow beds. But it was widely accepted that it was a predatory practice and one should take care not to be left alone with that Carol M., no matter how friendly and cheerful she might be.

WAS BRIAN GAY? THIS thought struck me like a tabloid headline as I pored over his medical records. There were two official MMPI tests conducted on him by psychiatrists over the years, and both indicated the raised masculine/feminine scale. This could be the terrible hidden secret I was searching for.

Yet, if it were true, was it a secret I wanted to uncover? I thought of my mother. Perhaps Brian had been gay and she had never known; or, even worse, she had suspected, but it was an issue neither of them could speak about.

At this point, my thoughts become unbearable, claustrophobic.

With my mother very much alive and perhaps reading this account one day, how can I be contemplating the most private details of her sexual life with my father? Certainly, in interviewing her, there are questions I don't want to ask, don't want to make her have to answer. I have no idea whether these are questions difficult for her to talk about, but I know that I would find it hard to listen.

In short, despite my apparent enlightened understanding of the infinite variety of sexual orientation among both the general population and my own friends, the idea of my father's mental illness being caused by repressed homosexuality represents the greatest possible scandal. Not only was the suicide itself an unimaginable secret; a homosexual tendency would take the story to a new level of hysteria.

On the one hand, this is the worst possible scenario, thinking of the supposed humiliation and shame it would visit upon my mother, and perhaps the family more generally. And to be bringing such a thing to light — even in a time in which all liberal-minded folk can discuss homosexuality openly and accept it in their friends' children, if not their own; a time when even Dick Cheney, whom no one would suspect of being liberal, accepts his lesbian daughter — how can I do this? What right do I have to be airing the family's dirty linen in public? What good will come of any of this?

I observe a part of me that feels ashamed of this entire project. Despite the contemporary American-inspired fashion for self-revelation, I find myself uneasy with my motives. I can still hear the traces of Tom's voice in my blood, and Frederick

Cecil before him: the *manly* way is to put one's chin up and get on with things, striding out into the world; why this *pathetic* need for introspection?

And yet, of course, I must be the hero of my own autobiography. Turning the tables, is there not something truly brave about confronting such taboos? So I flip-flop histrionically between these two positions, taking an emotional bet each way.

I am lured by the sheer drama of the 'closet gay' scenario. Even though I want it, for my mother's sake, to be a red herring, I am fascinated by its fevered possibilities.

Homosexuality in Australia in the 1940s and '50s was almost completely undercover. Men caught engaging in this type of behaviour were criminals, punishable by jail, not to mention deviants requiring professional psychological correction. Indeed, their sentencing usually involved some such combination of the stick of incarceration and the carrot of attempted psychiatric re-programming.

The newspapers of the day were replete with lurid stories. One such told of a lampshade shop at the end of Rundle Street in Adelaide where, after closing time, the blinds were drawn. The vice squad smashing through the rear door would discover, illuminated by a multitude of hanging shades, a homosexual soirée taking place in and around the soft furnishings.

Imagine if this was the sort of place Brian frequented, he being one of the lucky ones to slip away afterwards in the melee of arrests and shouting. Or if, perhaps, he observed secretly from the safety of the reflection in the draper's window across the street the smart young 'customers' arriving just on closing time and entering that door, whereas he himself couldn't quite pluck up the courage.

Among the University of Western Australia intellectual set in whose circle Brian moved, a number of men were generally assumed to be homosexual. John the opera-lover was one of them; Brian, apparently, was not.

In Perth in 2004, I interviewed two of the women from the intellectual set: Ailsa, who possibly coined the term, and Judy, who had been Brian's girlfriend.

Ailsa, retired from a distinguished career in child psychology, was an imposing character — the type of woman who would have scored highly on the masculine/feminine scale but then scoffed at its significance.

Judy, altogether softer and gentler, happened to live just across the road from Ailsa, and had been comparing memories of Brian with her in advance of my visit in an effort to help with my investigations. Judy empathised greatly with my desire to discover Brian, and had determined to become my ally in this quest. To this end, she put me on to Ailsa.

Brian, according to Judy, displayed every sign of heterosexuality in their relationship. Indeed, she claimed one of the reasons she called it off before a year was out was because she was afraid next thing she'd be pregnant, such was his enthusiasm to 'move things along'. He was not exactly macho in his style, she told me, but that only made him more attractive to her: the way he liked to talk and listen. That and his blond handsomeness; his sweet mix of poise and vulnerability.

Upon consideration, Ailsa joined Judy in dismissing the idea that Brian was homosexual. It was simply the case, they told me, that each person in their group at university, under the star of Freud, was open to the enlightened intellectual *consideration* of such matters. Coming from conservative middle-class families in the nearby suburbs, they enjoyed, in the safety and comfort of the university refectory, the feeling that they were cosmopolitan enough to be open to all sorts of possibilities that society as a whole may frown upon; open to all sorts of places they might *in theory* go, even if in practice they would soon be married off with children and lives as respectable as their parents'.

However, I wondered about John. He may have had a different view of Brian. As a gay man himself, he may have been privy to intimacies or conversations that the girls were never party to. He was still alive, retired after a long career in London.

When an opportunity arose for me to travel, I emailed him to introduce myself, and before long received a lengthy and charming email in reply, written in the well-crafted style of an old-fashioned longhand letter.

He told me that he would love to be able to help me and was more than happy to meet me in London, although for a reason he could not fathom he seemed to have a memory block about Brian, whom he acknowledged he knew well at university but strangely, and despite considerable effort, could not bring to mind. He retained, so he said, in lieu of any specific memory, only an overwhelmingly warm and positive feeling towards Brian. For an instant, as he read my letter, he said, he thought he saw Brian just as he was 50 years ago, but he realised in the next breath that the image of the man he had pictured was instead that of a certain rugby player named Carling with a 'g' who had featured in the newspapers several years earlier for his 'off-field activities'.

Despite these hesitations, about which he was refreshingly open, John said he was confident that just some small trigger or jolt would set his memories aflow.

I was excited and intrigued by my assignation. The idea of lunching with a suave old queen in his genteel London club — the man who might be able to provide the missing piece in the mystery of my father's life and death — was irresistibly exotic, a scene from a Graham Greene novel.

Since he had warned me that he would be flying out to Hong Kong the next day, and that he had a prior commitment to dinner with a young tennis-playing friend just back from a tournament in Amsterdam (John must have been nudging 80 — what kind of jetset life did he lead?), lunch a couple of hours after I had arrived at Heathrow on the long-haul flight from Melbourne was my only option.

I met him in a glassy state of jet-lagged tiredness, having wheeled my suitcase up and down a dozen Tube-station escalators, saving on the taxi fare.

John's club, the New Cavendish, stood on a quiet street just north of Marble Arch. It wasn't quite as swanky or grand as I had imagined. I was expecting something akin to the Adelaide Club, to which I had once been invited: a neo-colonial gentleman's preserve replete with stuffed tigers in display cabinets and a butler at your elbow as you sank into an oversized leather armchair. The New Cavendish was more like somewhere the parents in *Swallows and Amazons* would have visited in later life: a comfortable city refuge for country folk from the Home Counties and civil servants of a certain stature, or retired ones like John.

John arrived, dapper in a cravat and sports coat, with a strong flop of hair falling back upon itself. Only the cane he leant on gave away his age. He was splendidly pleased to pass a few hours with me, and ushered me to a small table near the almost-deserted bar. A pair of older women was taking tea at a table nearby; they spoke and ate discreetly, in the house style.

As soon as John lowered himself into his chair, he confessed, much to my disappointment, that he had failed to open the floodgates to any memories of Brian. Brian appeared to be, he said, erased entirely from his mind, and yet, he said, he knew so well that he knew him! 'What a puzzle, the human mind, is it not?' he mused apologetically, and offered me a sandwich.

I showed him several old photographs of Brian. He peered at each thoughtfully before shaking his head.

I wondered, in my jet lag, what was going on. Was he hiding something from me — exactly the story that I needed to uncover? I don't believe he was so good an actor. Or, remembering Freud, was he *unconsciously* repressing the memory of Brian for some or other reason? This was the most tantalising option, because it implicated in some shape or form my pet theory: homosexual desire. Did he fancy Brian, just like he did the tennis player? If so, did Brian welcome or acquiesce to, even fleetingly, his advances? Once I let my university classmate Andrew kiss me clumsily under the Hills hoist in our share-house garden in Adelaide when he was first coming out and I was drunk and open to experiment.

There could have been any number of variations of such a scene played out by John and Brian. Because if John had known Brian as well as he claimed, how could he have totally forgotten him? And if he hadn't known Brian that well, why had he bothered to meet with me at all? Merely out of curiosity, to pass an amusing summer's afternoon before his athletic young boyfriend returned from the Continent? He seemed so genuinely keen to help, and yet so unable, like someone desperate to communicate in a foreign language.

At the very least, I thought, I will get him to tell me what it felt like to be a homosexual man at that time and place, in Australia during and immediately after the Second World War. This is where his reserve truly surprised me. He would not make any open admission as to his sexuality. Ailsa and Judy had both spoken of him as gay, and he bore all the outward signs of being a *confirmed bachelor*, but it was as if, coming from that generation before Stonewall, he was not prepared to break a lifelong habit of discretion. He would happily talk about homosexuality, but only at the level of socio-historical generalities, ignoring each invitation that I artfully extended, or tried to artfully extend, to employ his own point of view. He maintained the objectivity of a tour guide in an historic house, and played what would have been known at the Cavendish as a resolutely straight bat.

At the end, John said to me, as he walked me the block to the Tube, 'My life has been like a shelf with lots of ornaments and things covered in dust. You've been helping me to dust.' He smiled fondly at me. It was as if Brian had been a keepsake that he had once owned but long ago misplaced and forgotten.

I bore him no ill feeling, he having been so unfailingly generous in demonstrating his inability to help me in my quest.

I thanked him for his time, and we waved as I descended into the hot burrow of the Tube. The trail had temporarily gone cold.

Chapter Nine

At university, particularly as exams approached, Brian fretted. It is normal to be nervous about exams, but he was noticeably worse than most. A friend of Brian's remembered taking him for a walk one day, through the bushland of Kings Park above the university, to try to calm him down. He had done well all year, his friend told him; he'd cope alright with the exam. I see them there, tramping through the sand with the river flickering through the trees below. Brian's shoulders hunched, he walks half a step behind, his attention fixed upon the pattern of twigs and stones, the ants that cross his path. He soaks up the reassurance of his friend greedily, but is always parched for more. The ideas won't stick; they drain away as from a leaky vessel torn by shifting currents.

When the dark thoughts hit, they come in skipping trails, laced one to the next to the next and dancing all around while he spins dizzy in their midst, trapped. Trapped. This is the heart of depression, as I understand it, as I have known it. The immobility that comes from having built in the mind walls on each side that block all pathways, and a low ceiling that blots out the open air above, so the only movement possible is a tunnel down.

Brian had heavy secrets. He believed there was something wrong with him — something that set him apart from all his classmates and his family. Other people coped and prospered; they laughed, unencumbered by shame and self-loathing. It was *easy* for other people. This thought he knew to be ridiculously simplistic and soaked with self-pity, and yet, and yet — look at them: they walk through life, and when their boots get muddy they rinse them off to start another day. He, on the other hand, stood frozen, sinking in the muck.

In case you're wondering how I know all this, of course I don't. But I am giving Brian everything I do know about depression. After all, it's just returning the favour. His genes have caused me more than enough trouble in this field from time to time. And you'll have to trust me here: *I know what he's thinking.* I know that I just said I didn't, but I do. After all, I have the chain of clues in the medical records, to which I'll shortly return, and I have the remembered whispers and observations of his friends and relations, at least those who haven't lost him in the meantime, like John. And I have the genes … Brian can't escape me now, I have him pinned: *I know what he's thinking.*

❧

One night, in second year at university, Brian took Judy to a 21st birthday party in Cottesloe. He picked her up from home in a borrowed car. Her parents could not fail to notice how clean and well-groomed a man he was. They were more than happy for him to come back afterwards and sleep the night on the verandah bed, rather than trek all the way home to Scarborough.

Perhaps on this evening, as on others, Brian and Judy walked barefoot on the beach and looked out across the water to the lights of Rottnest. She liked his gentleness towards her and his wit, but the intensity in his eyes frightened her.

Later, apparently, Brian wakes up with a familiar horror. His sheets are soaking cold around his middle; he has pissed himself again. Before dawn, he creeps down to the laundry trough in the lean-to with his sheets bundled up. It is not the first time that he has needed to do this. He works to soak and rinse them quietly, shuddering in the chill morning air when the pipes begin to whistle. So long as no one wakes, so long as no one comes out to find him here. *Brian? What on earth — ?* And he would stammer — he could not say, *I wet the bed.* How could he? A grown man — their daughter's suitor.

Judy remembers her shock that morning when she awoke to find his sheets already washed and hanging on the line, and him waiting fully dressed.

Why did he do this — was it nerves? It was a childhood problem he had never shaken. I have heard it said that Tom suffered the same affliction as a young man — this from the grandson of a woman with whom Tom once lodged for several months in Toodjay — but I'll bet Tom did not pass on this information to his son. Each generation's shameful secrets are hidden from the next.

The doctors called it 'nocturnal enuresis'. The doctors had names for everything, even their wildest surmises. It seems clear that Brian liked to visit doctors because he knew he had something wrong and wanted to find out what it was. He was patient and he was interested; he believed in their processes and techniques. He liked to put himself in their hands, to stretch back and feel the comfort of their authoritative knowledge wrap around him, gathering him up to fend off the demons, as perhaps he wished his mother could have. He liked to answer questions and tell his story again, even if it emerged as incoherent babble that neither he nor they could make sense of. The doctors sat in leather swivel chairs, fingering their stethoscopes or ashing their half-finished cigarettes, trying to decipher him, to see through him to a diagnosis.

In the beginning, they were circumspect. In 1946, Brian took himself to a navy medical officer at the Flinders Naval Hospital in Crib Point. The conversation was one-sided: Brian talked, the doctor listened. He noted down on his pad: 'Complains of burning sensation over bladder area on passing water. 7 weeks ago — contact.' Contact?

Sifting through the bureaucratic traces of various consultations, I find the ugly medical language — dysuria, micturition, enuresis — peppered with enigmatic plot-points. A year later, a different doctor had written: 'Dysuria'. I look it up. It means difficult or painful pissing. 'Dysuria came on about 12 months ago after he thought he may have had intercourse.'

So 'contact' means intercourse? Even the second doctor couldn't bring himself to say 'sexual'; no doubt this says more about the society he lived in than his own character. But what about this: 'he thought he may have had' intercourse. Well, did you have it, Brian, or did you not? Where lies the ambiguity? In the nature of the act you were engaged in, your memory, or — ?

What were you up to, Brian? Something illicit or forbidden? Were you worried you had contracted VD? The tests came up with nothing. Was this the night I've heard about from Peter Graham when, on weekend R and R, you appeared drunk as a skunk in Collins Street, Melbourne, and vomited in the gutter? Did your navy mates from HMAS *Cerberus* introduce you to some ladies of their acquaintance up in Little Lonsdale Street, or through a door off a back lane near the station? Or was it indeed some homosexual experimentation — does this explain your haziness of language? *I think I may have had* — the truth is, you were so blind-drunk, you can't remember what you did, can you? Your malady is guilt, father! I wish you could have seen that.

'I consider his symptoms to be due to his worry about exposure,' wrote the second navy doctor, sitting in the cramped sick bay on board HMAS *Cowra*, anchored in the South Pacific. He found 'no evidence of organic lesion'. Brian's many symptoms shuffled by like carriages on a Ferris wheel: he felt giddy, had a 'swimming head', suffered from 'shivering' and 'nervousness', pains 'in the spleen region'. Not to mention, as the carnival gathered pace: 'Burning feeling in urethra. Pain at base of penis. Pain in testes. Pain in chest. Headache. Tight feeling across base of neck and tightness in throat.' No wonder the doctor could observe, against the gentle rocking of the ship, a 'fine tremor' in Brian's hands.

BRIAN SHUDDERS AWAKE at night and tugs on the light-string to illuminate himself and make sure he isn't dead.

THE DOCTORS CONSIDERED the possibility of malaria contracted on the corvette in the tropics. They conducted tests on Brian's heart, spleen, lungs, throat, urethra, testes, and blood, but uncovered only the startlingly good health of youth. But doctor, he insisted, I feel I am 'never quite up to the mark'; my 'tongue is always dirty'. He wanted to know what this could mean. The doctor, I suggest, chewed at the end of his fountain pen. He certainly clutched at more hypotheses: 'testinal parasites e.g. Hookworm??? Pulm T.B.?' More tests were called for, undertaken. But none would discover a physiological cause.

Each time an external pathogen was struck off the list of suspects, Brian found himself more isolated. Another spotlight rounded on him. No microbes, parasites, or viruses assaulted him. Not even a hitherto unrecognised congenital weakness lurked in his body, causing his heartbeat to be arrhythmic or his immune system weak. Doctor after doctor looked him in the eye; they didn't have to say it: *There is nothing wrong with you, Brian.* Leading to the obvious conclusion: *It is all in the mind.* At which point, his father's gun-barrel gaze intruded into his imaginings, pierced him in his sights across the dining table, and fired off a volley: *Just snap out of it, son.*

Most of the time, Brian passed; he presented as normal. He

joined his university friends skylarking in the hot pool by the river. He dressed up for the end-of-year Agriculture barn dance. He went to see Jack Carmichael and his sister in their jazz trio in the club on Mounts Bay Road. He squeezed into the back seat of a friend's car for the run down Stirling Highway to gatecrash, just for fun, the party of a final-year girl from English in a house above the cliffs at Mosman Park. He ran down into the river to skinny-dip among the jellyfish in the moonlight.

But every now and then the pressure of his thoughts began to swamp him. In August 1948, he was admitted to the Hollywood General Repatriation Hospital for returned servicemen, which was situated, conveniently, just up the road from the university. It was to be the first of many such sojourns over the next 15 years. According to the records, the complaint he presented with was, on the surface, trivial: 'becomes tired and nervy easily'. After 22 days in hospital — in which his urine and blood were tested once again, his sinuses X-rayed, his ears, nose, and throat inspected — despite there being no explicit note of any psychiatric examination, two doctors, in preparation for his discharge, concluded with a humble new diagnosis: 'Anxiety state (mild).' The official finger at last pointed definitively at his mind.

With questions of the cost of hospitalisation and further treatment surfacing, the Repatriation Board was asked to assess Brian's case. Mr Taylor, the deputy commissioner, signed the letter, accepting that, after 'full consideration', Brian's 'nervous condition' had been found attributable to his war service. Notwithstanding that he had been demobilised from the navy with a clean bill of health, and had signed a form to that effect, his file was now to be officially reopened. A pension, Mr Taylor hastened to add to his opening sentence, would not be payable, since the doctors advised that Brian was still fit to study and embark on a career; however, medical expenses would be covered by the department.

Friends visited Brian in hospital. Doris, I imagine, brought him food and new pyjamas, sometimes flowers from the garden. She got to know where the sink was, for changing the water in the vase. He joked with each of his visitors so nobody would worry. Exactly what was the matter with him remained somewhat obscure; but some things, it seemed, were better not discussed.

In point of fact, it was in failing to adhere to this latter maxim that Brian slipped up with the intellectual set, his Psychology friends, according to the doctors. He *delved* into things too much.

He emerged quite well from that first stint in hospital, but a year later again consulted a doctor upon, the notes said, 'getting depressed, nervy and jumpy, & not concentrating well'. Upon examination, this Dr Wilson concluded that: 'Physically he is sound, but is getting introspective & mixed up in the various theories of life and religion at the university.' This is certainly not a reference to his Agriculture studies. By way of treatment, Dr Wilson adopted the benevolent paternal role that Brian craved in the emotional absence of his own father: 'I had a long talk to him,' noted Wilson, '& told him that I was sure things would straighten out if he maintained confidence & stopped worrying about various theories & ideas outside his work.' Brian having left the room, Wilson concluded his comments crisply with a single word: 'Neurosis.'

Judy, Brian's girlfriend, knew she would have to leave him, for fear not only of falling pregnant but moreover of that heaviness he carried. Besides, she had a ready excuse: her mother had told her that she would have to fall in love with 20 men before she found the one to marry, and Brian was just the first. In this sense, it was a simple question of mathematics.

Brian, from what they tell me, loved the way conversations with Judy, or with all his pals in the refectory, could *delve* into the strange abysses of the mind, since so many psychological conundrums bounced around in his own head. But he could also see the doctor's point, perhaps: that this was a kind of fatal attraction, a lure to spin deeper into the trap of madness rather than to negotiate a way out. If he could only think through the puzzle properly. What *was* wrong with him, after all?

I see them in the university refectory: it is late in the afternoon, as the staff clean up and only Brian's table lingers. He tells his Psychology friends secrets about his wartime experiences that he would afterwards have trouble telling anyone. As they thrash through the thickets of Freud's theories on sexuality, repression, and trauma, conversation inevitably flows to musings upon their own experience. In a kind of intellectual spin-the-bottle, each member of the circle peels off another layer of personal disclosure.

When it comes Brian's turn, he says, haltingly, 'There was a time — on a jetty.' He tells them: a jetty in the moonlight, in the Solomon Islands. 'Something happened to me there,' he tells them. He finds it hard to say the words exactly. He is floating apart from his body, above the wooden table. His ears are humming, his mouth is dry.

As the story is relayed to me by Judy, and in other versions by other friends of Brian, the details slip and shimmer. I believe he said it was a gang of American sailors, says one. It may have been kitchen hands involved, says another. At night in the Solomons, the minesweeper moored at the dock, and the sailors went to shore for R and R. Rest and Recreation. Rape.

Gang rape. The stories agree on this, although they avoid the words themselves, just as I do when I finally raise the subject with my mother. Has she heard this story? Of an *assault* in the navy? Had he ever talked about this with her?

She looks blank. No. She hasn't heard it. But she says she's not surprised to hear it now. It could well make sense. It could well be true. But I can see it's not an area in which she's keen to *delve*. After all, she was never in that set. We come from a long line of *non-delvers*; I've said this before, in one way or another. Brian was the odd one out.

He was worried he might have enjoyed the rape, Judy told me. Apparently, the literature asserts that this guilt is widely observed in sufferers of sexual assault: what did *I* do to bring this on? Did I *want* this to happen? Brian was very fair, with big blue eyes (just like Frank on the big screen); this, Judy said, made him an object of attraction for homosexual men. They would approach him on the street or in a bar, she said. It happened to my brother too, she said, 'He was also blond.' This direct correlation between blondness and male homosexual desire is something new to me. But perhaps I am reading what she said too literally.

What could be worse than to be gang-raped *and* to think you might have enjoyed it? To suffer such a violent humiliation and take pleasure in it — this is perversity in the extreme. My mind is colonised by old memories of the Rainer Werner Fassbinder film *Querelle*, adapted from the novel of Jean Genet. The intoxicating aroma of male hard-bodied sweat, and on a tropical jetty in the moonlight, all those young sailor-boys with their Marlon Brando T-shirts, caps, and boots. The bollards shaped like giant phalluses. A liquid ocean made of plastic, à la Fellini (or is this detail just my fantastic blurring together of two films?). The rhythmic sounds of the waves against the distant shore, the grinding of ropes, spitting onto hands. Laughter and the tongue-kissing of liquor bottles. I can't help but paste this fantasy onto Brian, even though nothing may be further from the truth.

This is the technicolour gory bit I was saving for the climax: the scene on the jetty, the key moment of unravelling from which every thread of Brian's life before and after winds, to and from his doom; the most expensive scene in the opera. The settings are spectacular, the sky tinged blood-red as dawn appears in the clouds. Fishing folk, subsistence extras, prepare to launch into their gliding canoes somewhere on the edges of the picture. Brian is alone on the lower section of the jetty where they left him, curled up on his side like a conch shell, his mind spiralling away. The quintessential victim. He's missed the curfew — reveille will sound and find him missing. The salty smell of tropical barnacles brings him back to life. He remembers the Indian Ocean at Scarborough Beach, the way it drops off suddenly into the abyss as you walk out towards the waves. The hot sand on your feet, scanning the horizon for a shark fin. His lips are thick and crusty with dehydration; his body aches. If he's careful, he can sneak back onto the *Cowra* without attracting attention. He will find himself in his bunk again, shielding his face from humiliation with a blanket. In the boxy, claustrophobic mess for breakfast, the conversation will take place in sideways glances.

Rape is so common that this event can't be considered unimaginable or inexplicable. Every war, we're told, brings a grinning, ugly queue of them. Lads being lads and doing what lads do, pissed and hot with pent-up fear. Could be me next; could be any of us. But we're in the gang. Better shove than be shoved.

The final time Brian reports to the doctor on the *Cowra*, first thing on the morning of 27 November 1946, the ailment he presents will be more obvious than those previous. 'Lacerated right eye,' notes the doctor. *And tell me, how did you come by that nasty gash, able seaman?*

Brian, my Brian, is acutely aware that the whole crew across the ship has paused to listen for his answer. *I was bashed. They bashed me on the jetty. They* — of course he cannot say it, any of it. He is too afraid. That is not the way the world works. He does not have Frank Sinatra playing him; indeed, those boys on the jetty, those Yanks, it may have been they who were the Rat Pack. After all, those guys were the heroes in their own minds. The conquerors of war; testosterone and bootlegged corn whisky. Singing, dancing, pissing, fucking, bashing. Oh, and sweet camaraderie. What we learnt at boys' school: tunnel ball, where the PE teacher whipped your bum with his whistle string if you were too slow; where the social studies teacher crushed your toes under your desk with his shoe if he saw fit; where the weak were to be hounded and abused —

Brian shrugs away the scene. 'Fell off mess deck table,' the doctor writes. None of his business, anyway.

REVIEWING THE TRANSCRIPT of the interview that I conducted with Judy in Perth those few years ago, I realise the extent to which her version of Brian's dramatic revelation differed from that of Ailsa. Judy, in fact, didn't mention the refectory scene; the scene she retained was an intimate one, alone with Brian, where his story surfaced fleetingly, triggered by the emotional tenor of the conversation that they happened to be having concerning their relationship. She remembered noticing how highly charged the memory was for Brian, how evidently shocking, how he could allude to it only via a series of clues and fragments, never even mentioning directly its sexual, let alone *homo*sexual, nature. She told me that only over the course of the next 15 years, as she returned again and again to this conversation in her mind, was she able to piece the jigsaw together and belatedly decipher what it may have been that he was trying to communicate.

My story is built from air, quite literally from the breath of voices and the gaps between them, on the shifting haze of memories.

SOMETHING ALWAYS NAGGED at me. What of Brian's shipmates on the *Cowra*? What if, over half a century later, an eyewitness was still alive who could testify once and for all as to *the incident*?

Believing that the chances of finding anyone were slim, I posted an advertisement in the magazine of the Returned Serviceman's League.

Within a few weeks, I had several friendly responses, and it became evident a lively if diminishing network of *Cowra* veterans were motoring into the new century. They all remembered Brian, more or less. They sent me cheerful photographs of shipside days, and spoke to me on the phone. Some preferred handwritten letters, while others dashed off emails. Ted asked me if Brian had received the four service medals owed to him, and explained how I could apply for them; Peter enquired if my mother had her Veteran's Gold Card. Finally, I broached the difficult issue at hand.

Peter said it was unimaginable that such a thing could have happened in the confines of the *Cowra* without everybody knowing. His tone was calm and measured, not defensive.

Later, another letter arrived, from a man named Fred, formerly an Able Seaman with Brian. The two of them, he said, were among a dozen or so lads who had lived at close quarters, eaten at the same table, the whole year of 1946. Fred, like Peter, had no knowledge whatsoever of the story of sexual assault. However, he said that even now he remembers Brian reasonably clearly, and recalls noticing, just prior to the *Cowra's* return to Sydney in 1946, that Brian began acting strangely. He became very quiet and vacant, said Fred.

Fred reckons that he and others around him were concerned at the time for Brian — the more so because they had, not long before, witnessed another of their shipmates *go troppo*, as they then called it, and thereafter the unfortunate man's removal from the ship and dispatch south to hospital. Similar cases were heard of, too, he told me, on their sister ships among the corvette minesweepers.

But Brian never 'broke', said Fred, and after the crew went their separate ways at Christmas, 1946, he never heard of, or from, him again. This was not unusual — Western Australia was, after all, so very far away.

For Fred, as for each of the old *Cowra* crew who contacted me, my news of Brian's suicide — arriving after all of these years — came as a shock. In reply, each expressed to me his condolences with great respect and tenderness.

No corroboration, then. Instead, those few words: *acting strangely*, *quiet*, and *vacant*.

એ

At university, Brian felt the pressures in his mind mount again. He called for a local doctor, whose notes, in their brevity, sound harsher than he surely would have meant: 'Mr B. F. Carlin ... obviously a psychopathic case requiring treatment. He tells me he is entitled to treatment at 110 Hosp.'

Note the specific turn of phrase: 'he tells me he is entitled'. This sense of entitlement, and the quality of services freely available to ex-servicemen, may have contributed to Brian's problems, according to my aunt Alison. She believes it was too easy for Brian to have himself admitted into hospital. She believes, as did many others, that these recurring hospital visits and the treatments that accompanied them only made him worse, not better. The more the scab is picked, the more it bleeds. If only he could have stopped focusing on his distress, it may have receded rather than enveloped him.

But into hospital he went for another month, once again interrupting his studies. By now, the doctors were concentrating on his mind rather than his body. Brian was interviewed first by one psychiatrist, then another. He wanted to talk forever, to untangle the knot of thoughts that kept out sleep. But his ideas bounced back and forth like squash balls, always returning to the same place at the centre of the court.

The doctors listened to his ramblings, and quietly formulated new theories according with the latest medical insights of the day. Psychiatrist number one detected in Brian a 'compulsive element which prevents his voluntary actions and occupations'; he also suspected 'schizoid elements'. Psychiatrist number two agreed with the 'compulsive' tag and added the words 'hypochondriacal elements' and 'marked Obsessional neurosis'.

Brian no doubt would have been morbidly fascinated to have been privy to their scribblings. As for me, I wondered what to make of this cocktail of diagnoses. Could all these elements fit together to form a coherent understanding of his state of mind? Were they anything more than a series of informed guesses?

For the first time, the doctors proposed Electro-Convulsive Treatment (ECT): shock therapy. Brian told them he was 'quite willing to be so treated'; after all, he was always open to whatever the experts deemed best.

ECT, if you believe Wikipedia, is 'a psychiatric treatment in which seizures are induced by passing electricity through the brain'. Electrodes are attached to the patient's head, and a current switched on for several seconds. In Brian's time, the procedure was performed without an anaesthetic. The force of the electric shock convulsed his body and rendered him unconscious. In the initial series, he received ECT twice a week for a fortnight. Hospital staff observed in the following days that he was 'frequently confused about facts'. However, since confusion and memory loss are commonly reported side effects of ECT, this was considered normal.

An Italian psychiatrist named Ugo Cerletti developed ECT in the 1930s in line with a theory that a 'natural antagonism' between schizophrenia and epilepsy meant that the artificial prompting of an epileptic-style convulsion would work to mitigate schizophrenic tendencies in the brain. Similar ideas have been traced back to the medieval belief that schizophrenic symptoms were a sign of the devil dwelling in the afflicted mind: healers then prescribed drastic remedies, such as lowering patients into lakes in nets, or whipping them with chains to shock Satan from his hidey-hole.

As early as the mid-18th century, the newly discovered phenomenon of electricity was tested as a more efficient form of shock. The theologian John Wesley was an early advocate, writing in his journal on 9 November 1756: 'Having procured an apparatus, I ordered several persons to be electrified who were ill of various disorders; some of whom found an immediate, some a gradual cure ...'

Cerletti's antagonism theory eventually proved baseless, but

ECT remained a popular therapy. Psychiatrists believed that they saw evidence of its benefits, but ideas never settled as to how, and on which complaints, it acted. Thus, like many of the treatments Brian would receive, ECT was in effect experimental: a cutting-edge psychiatric technology, it had only been taken up widely in clinical practice in the preceding five years, or ten at most. Given a paucity of other treatment options and the excitement generated by reports of good results achieved elsewhere, Brian's doctors decided it was worth giving ECT a go to see what would happen.

❧

Here is Brian now with the western sun seeping into the psychiatric ward at Hollywood, its heat upon the bricks outside. Hospital has become a cocoon in which to wrap himself. He gives himself over to the ministrations of the staff, and wonders about his sanity.

He likes the pretty nurse who arrives in the afternoons. If only she would sit and hold his hand and stroke it all night, until he could fall asleep. But she bustles, like the others, stopping only to take a measurement, supply a medication, put down a meal.

He shouldn't be here, he tells himself; he should be coping. What must all his friends be saying? But his being here means everyone can understand the full weight of what afflicts him. He isn't making it up. It is something to be taken seriously. On the one hand, it is his fault; on the other hand, it is not his fault. His thoughts slide back and forth like a lab rat tiptoeing up and down a seesaw.

He is not quite right; he can feel it in his bones. If only there were another test they could do that would come up with a conclusive answer. He could relax. They could apply a medicine in tablet form.

The doctor suggests shock therapy again. It is a matter of honour for him to accept. Tom would be proud of him, being brave enough to face the terror of it *like a man* as they strap him to the gurney and clamp the electrodes to his skull. The doctor says that Brian's thoughts are in a rut, digging themselves deeper. The shock treatment will blast them out. His brain will have a chance to start off fresh.

On the gurney, as they ready the machine, he has to concentrate so as not to panic. These men and women fussing about could easily be executioners, wiring him up for the death that would take him off their hands. Not for the first time, he considers whether his death would be a sweet relief for one and all. But is he not himself in training in a branch of rational science? He has faith, after all, in medical methods and techniques, does he not? His thoughts: once again, not only a rut, a jumble.

On the gurney, he closes his eyes, grips his teeth together, and submits to his fate. The doctor flicks the switch, or turns the knob, or pulls the Gothic lever, or does whatever necessary to open up the sluicegates and let the silken surge of electricity flood through Brian's brain.

Chapter Ten

We grew up in Perth in the 1960s and '70s in a suburb bounded by swamps and sand dunes. To the west, the bush was fenced off for an army rifle range where perhaps Tom's ghost patrolled, kicking spent shells and barking orders.

To the north lay the sandy, wooded hills of Bold Park. To the south, in the hollow behind the Lakeway drive-in, was the reed-choked swamp latterly christened Lake Claremont, from where the blackfellas had been moved on years ago to make way for private-school playing grounds and a rubbish tip on which a civic golf course was later built — 18 holes of green undulation.

On the eastern side, behind the bus stop where we waited each morning to catch the 206 to school, the dunes stretched up a hill capped in all its shadowy splendour by the Graylands

Mental Hospital. The loony bin. A magnificent collection of 19th-century brick buildings rearing up above the tangled gums and surrounded by a high wall.

The loony bin was not somewhere you ever approached: as with all the great asylums, it was designed to isolate its inmates from society at large, for their sanctuary and our safety. Our peace of mind. It gnawed away at the edges of our vision, a threatened destination in playground games, an eerie backdrop to our sunny suburbs. Who wandered in the grounds in the shadows of those buildings? Who looked out from the high windows? Did they dress in white smocks and shuffle along dim corridors, shafts of sunlight striking the dribble on their chins? At night, the mad unseen orchestra with its terrifying roars and groans, its sad melody of ravings — if the wind swung to the east, would we hear it drifting in above the sleeping houses, just as we heard in bed the singing gear changes of the speedway from the showgrounds every Friday night?

Later, I imagined Brian in the asylum, among the lost souls and the sunken. I pictured him as the normal one whose tics and deformations were invisible unless one peered into his eyes and glimpsed the flickering despair. I saw him consigned to this Edwardian mansion of the damned, receiving his shock treatment from the local Dr Mengele on the stainless-steel gurney, and stumbling out afterwards for basket-weaving.

If Brian was in Hollywood Hospital instead, a more banal reality — low-slung fingers of red-brick sheltering in a suburb lined with blossoms — the idea of the asylum nevertheless hovered in the air. The psychiatric ward at Hollywood was locked off from its other sections: visitors could not stroll through casually as they did elsewhere. It was a secret place where the incomprehensible dwelt, where family shames were hidden.

Brian came out of his spell in hospital in 1950 feeling better, and returned to university. Everyone was hopeful that whatever was wrong had been dealt with and that he could now get along with life. As he bounced cheerfully back into classes, his friends remained quietly mystified as to his problems.

Brian wanted to move into the university hostel, which made special provision to house ex-servicemen. His study allowance of three pounds and ten shillings afforded him the luxury to choose to live away from home. The bus ride each day from Scarborough to the campus in Crawley was long and tedious; he would have told Doris he'd be better able to study without it. He'd be better able to study without the distractions of Noel and Andrew looking over his shoulder and sniggering at his botanical sketches under the desk-lamp in the sleep-out. I expect Doris would have talked to Tom and he would have seen the logic, although by this point he had lost the power to control the actions of his eldest son.

Life at the hostel was a lark. There was a men's wing and a women's wing, and strict rules against fraternising in the other gender's bedrooms, save on Sunday afternoons when groups were permitted to gather until 8.00 p.m. Men and women met for meals in the central dining room, with supper at nine in the evening being the time for relaxed socialising after studies wound up for the day.

The men, many affecting the grizzled charm of the returned warrior, ideally accessorised with leather jacket and second-hand motorbike, mingled at the tables with the bright-eyed country girls. This is where Brian met Joan Stewart, my mother.

'I KNEW what I was getting into,' says my mother. This cannot be entirely true; she means she was under no illusion that he had not suffered occasional mental problems. But she cannot have known that, in living with him, she would have to learn to cope with the constant ebb and flow of dread.

'I thought that I could save him,' she once told me, when she first began to talk about him after all those years. The tears welled in her eyes, the long-reserved emotion so ready to erupt.

Joan's father, Jack, advised her in the lead-up to the marriage to consider the matter carefully. However, when upon reflection her feelings and decision were unchanged, he gave his blessing.

Jack as a father was cut from different cloth to Tom. Of Scottish stock, his style was stoic, quiet, and measured rather than domineering. His wife, Barbara, had only one complaint against him: he took so long about communicating — to respond in conversation, to take his turn when playing bridge. Cautious and deliberate, he would answer a question long after she had forgotten asking it.

(My mother — what will I call her in this story? Mum? Joan?)

Joan, this woman whom Brian met across the table at the university hostel, studied Agriculture, just like he did. This was almost unheard of for a girl, but she was a smart girl from a farm who couldn't think what else to do at university. She had considered doing nursing at the training college, but her father said that, with marks as good as hers and a University Exhibition award, she was too clever to be a nurse: if she wanted a career of a medical persuasion, she should train to be a doctor. To which she replied, 'But I don't want to be a doctor.'

Having skipped a grade in primary school, owing to her ease with sums and sentences and everything else that the teacher put in front of her, Joan finished high school at 16 and, feeling too young to make an entrance on the adult stage of university, stayed home for a year. She was happy to work on the farm, although out in the paddocks and the sheds with the sheep and the dogs rather than in the house, getting dirty alongside her father and a local boy whom he employed called Gres. Gres, she fancied.

Opportunities to meet boys were few and far between, living in the country. Joan made her own dress, she tells me, 'a nice red and white spotty one', for one of the dances held in Kojonup. All the girls sat along the edges with their parents and hoped that someone — one of those scrubbed-up gangly boys — would come along for a dance. A foxtrot or a quickstep, or a bit of old-time Pride of Erin. If chosen for the supper dance or the last dance, you knew 'you really were something — you had someone who had asked you for the dance'.

In the summer, as happened every year, the district's self-appointed matchmaker, Mrs Potts, rowed selected groups of boys and girls across the Denmark inlet to the holiday cabins belonging to herself and Brigadier Potts for the purpose of orchestrating suitable future marriages.

Five girls and five boys were invited to spend a week and get to know each other. The parents knew that Mrs Potts would never allow anything untoward. Mrs Potts plied her teenage charges with large quantities of scones, jam, bacon, and eggs, to fortify them in her own image, before dispatching them on organised walks through the scrubland.

It was here that Joan and Gres 'teamed up', as Joan describes it, much to the annoyance of the voluminous Mrs Potts, who had pencilled Gres beside her daughter's name.

Arriving at university, Joan had no thought of a career: perhaps she could marry Gres and use any professional skills learnt in Agriculture to help out on a farm of their own?

Joan came from a *good family*. Her father, Jack, trained to be an engineer like his own father, John, who was a wealthy and well-respected gentleman about Perth before the strange incident in 1928 at Gibraltar — but I shall return to this.

Barbara grew up galloping horses across the fields of her cousin's estate in the middle of Claremont, where an elite school now stands.

Newlyweds Jack and Barbara took up farming at about the same time as Tom and Doris, but a windfall on Jack's father's sandalwood shares bought them into a district with far better prospects, south on the highway towards Albany. They were always going to be in a stronger position to see out the Great Depression. Nevertheless, listening to the stories, they were hardly landed gentry. They churned their own butter, baked their own bread, grew their own fruit and vegetables, and killed their own meat. A photo shows Barbara standing on a wooden trailer in a broad-brimmed hat and long skirt, bending her back to pitch hay.

Joan, the middle child of three, was the bright one. During the war, there wasn't enough petrol to drive the five miles to school, so Joan and Marg, her elder sister, took correspondence lessons from their mother in the mornings before running off down to the creek, where each staked out their favourite climbing tree.

When the girls grew older and baby brother Graeme came along, they rode bicycles to school, Joan perched precariously atop the full-size boy's bike that would one day be Graeme's. Once launched on her way, she couldn't stop; her feet waved in mid-air beyond the pedals, and if she skidded on the sandy track and fell off, or was waylaid by the springtime temptation of setting off the trigger plants, there was no way up again. She preferred to ride the horse, instead, and tether it up at the post office for Mrs Gale to mind.

Saturdays, the family harnessed up the horse and cart, took chops and potatoes, and journeyed to the far corners of the farm to burn the cleared scrub and fumigate rabbits. Marg and Joan set huge traps for rabbits, too, but to Marg fell the job of wringing their necks.

Every month or two, they travelled into the Big Town, bumping up and down on the back of the ute, huddled under homemade dust jackets to protect their Sunday-best. In Katanning there was a shop splendid beyond belief, in which a cord system whizzed money back and forth across the ceiling.

As to the story of John, the grandfather — my great-grandfather — it is not something *good families* spoke about, then or now, and certainly Joan didn't know of it growing up. It wavers in the margins of the family history in vague and insubstantial form, thus:

One day, or night, off the coast of Gibraltar, while returning home from a family trip to England, John Stewart jumped overboard — leapt from the ship's side and disappeared into the waves. Down he went, to sink without a trace in the family history of solidity and success.

How strange to find an echo of Brian so unexpectedly near at hand. I look at Great-grandfather Stewart sitting stiffly proud and upright in a family photo taken in the 1920s, his hat across his lap. This is not a man who will commit suicide, surely? But show me a picture of a man who will commit suicide. Most of them, unfortunately, are better actors.

I discover, too, that John Stewart was not the only person on Joan's side of the family to suffer, it seems, from depression. Jack's sister, my Great-aunt Margaret, who never married and lived with her widowed mother until the latter's death, would often have spells, I'm told, during which she was 'indisposed; not seeing people'. If visitors came to the house, her mother would say, 'Margaret's not feeling well today ...' and conversation would pause a moment to allow everyone to clutch at pleasantries and biscuits.

These matters lie in the shade waiting for other stories to obscure them. The guardians of propriety say we cannot be sure: perhaps Joan's grandfather fell from the boat in an uncanny accident? Perhaps none of this ever really happened. What good will come, what good will come? Can we not choose the past we prefer?

Be that as it may, for those of us with a penchant for melodrama … a suicide, depression, mental illness on this side of the family, too! From no suicides to begin with, in the innocence of childhood, to inexplicable despair on all sides.

What kind of genetic cocktail is this whipping up? How does one make sense of the memories one is bequeathed, or from which one is disinherited? But perhaps these stories are not so uncommon after all. Perhaps most families would uncover them if they went looking.

Take a deep breath.

～

Joan and Brian: falling in love over supper at the university hostel.

Joan excelled at university — too much, in fact. At the end of her first year, a scandal erupted behind closed doors: she had topped her class in the exams. The Agriculture faculty staff agreed it would do nothing for their reputation to announce that a girl had attained the highest marks, so the grades were gently reassessed to ensure that one of the male students nudged her out.

Brian was a charmer, all the girls agreed. He looked so elegant with his ties and tweed jackets, his tall frame, handsome eyes, and blond hair. He liked, even preferred, the company of women; there wasn't the prospect of an arm-wrestle in every conversation. Joan was sharp, as everyone knew, but also practical and straightforward, the antithesis to the wild girls and dreamers of the intellectual set. She wasn't one to wander deep into psychological analyses or metaphysical debates — and perhaps Brian could see, with the advice of the doctors in his ears, that this was what he needed.

They began to go out together. They caught the bus up the highway to the Windsor cinema to see a double feature, or bathed together in the hot pool in Dalkeith. Sometimes Brian borrowed the family car and they went for drives, stopping in a car park to watch the lights from the ships moored out in Gauge Roads and the lighthouse blinking across the water. They cuddled on the beach, bought hamburgers at the Eats kiosk with the flashing neon sign in North Cottesloe. Coming to the end of his final year, Brian helped organise the Agriculture barn dance. He and Joan attended arm in arm.

Brian invited Joan home to meet his family at the house in Scarborough. She witnessed with shock the painful and repeated dinner-table scenes of Tom humiliating Doris. And if not Doris, it was Noel, the *slow* brother, the *weak* one who couldn't play football *or* surf *or* pass his tests at school. Joan watched Brian disappearing into silence.

'I knew he had problems,' she continues. 'I went to see him at the hospital; it wasn't like it was a big secret. But he didn't talk about it much; in those days, one didn't talk about it … I didn't feel I could talk about it with anyone. Not with Mum and Dad, because I didn't want to worry them.' Her eyes, even at this distance of 50 years, are delicate with tears.

'I probably didn't ask enough, I probably wasn't a very good listener,' she says, as the tangled weight of regret bears down. The first thing she asked Eric the day Brian died: 'Was it my fault? Was it my fault?' As if, always, there was something she should have done, she could have done. But — what?

'I just thought it was something *he* had to do; there didn't seem very much that anyone else could do ...' It was a problem that he had to work out, its nature opaque, its dimensions unknowable. And was it not, surely, a flimsy thing that would one day blow away in the air? Where did it exist? Only as whispers in his mind. Would not their young love be strong enough to banish any nightmares?

There was no big proposal scene, or if there was it has slipped away from memory. Nevertheless, it became clear between them, as Brian approached his graduation, that they would bide their time until Joan had finished her own degree, and make plans to marry thereafter.

Upon graduating, Brian took up a job in January 1951 with the West Australian government's Department of Agriculture as a district advisor. They posted him to the research station at Wongan Hills, three or four hours' north-east of Perth. As a salaried officer of the Crown, he now had the wherewithal to sign up, on hire purchase, for a brand new Morris, in which he could sweep down to the city on weekends to stay at Scarborough, and take Joan out from the hostel to parties or home for the family Sunday roast.

Within 18 months, the department transferred Brian to its Mount Barker office in the state's far south.

He showed a lot of promise in his work. He could see a future as a wheat and sheep advisor, stamping a worthwhile footprint on the world. The farmers were crying out for help, a lot of them; they needed to be told about pasture and crop management, basic fertiliser programs, disease control. To be the local agriculture advisor was like being the parish priest: people hung upon your every word, and when they got in a mess you could step in to dig them out.

Brian saw so many exciting results coming out of scientific experiments and trials; they just needed someone to explain them to the farmers. New techniques would achieve vastly improved yields. He would be the one to do it. He would be the champion. He would do better, and be better, than anyone had hoped; he would be perfect, loved, and respected, he would —

My aunt Alison's parents happened to live on a farm at Mount Barker at that time. Alison told me that one day Brian turned up at the back door in a distressed state, having walked *four miles across country* from the neighbouring farm where he was staying. Something had occurred with two male associates on this other farm — a dispute? a taunt? something physical? He couldn't say exactly, but it had propelled him into fleeing.

He rested a couple of days with Alison's parents, talking, drinking tea, walking up and down the hills. They, non-conformists — the father, a farmer and former teacher who would rather read poetry than shoot kangaroos; the mother, a broad-minded, educated woman — made no demands upon him.

Alison's story continued. 'I am afraid that I am dying,' Brian confided to Alison's mother in her kitchen. 'What should I do?' His irrational ideas poured out with the tea. 'We used to have a light bulb with a switch on a string,' he told her, 'and when I woke up in the night and thought I was dying, I would have to pull the string to turn the light on to stop from dying; and when I couldn't reach the string from bed, I had to attach a tie to the string to make it longer …'

Alison's mother listened to everything he had to say, no matter how crazy it was. This was what he loved. She had no fear of his gushing thoughts. He reminded her of her friend Betty Dovey's husband, who lived in town. Betty's man had also been to war, and had come home troubled and depressed.

When Brian told Alison's mother about his fears in the night, she said to him gently: 'Well then, when that happens, why don't you just lie down and die?' Whether or not he could see what she was getting at, for that moment, sitting in that kitchen, he felt better, filled up again with hope. But he was so fragile. She could see it in his eyes. Afterwards, it would take just a breath, the proverbial butterfly flapping its wings, for his strength of mind to drain away.

ONCE MORE, Brian appealed to the doctors for help. In May 1953, they admitted him briefly to Hollywood Hospital for further tests: perhaps chronic malaria was still an underlying cause of his mysterious symptoms? An intensive course of nicotinic acid was prescribed. But the medicos were increasingly frustrated.

At the hospital, Dr C. described him as 'rather undecided and dependent. Appears as if he would be content to remain indefinitely, asking questions in a hesitant manner and not considering any answer that [does] not suit him'.

A psychologist asked Brian to complete another MMPI

test, on which the scores indicated that his anxiety level was 50 per cent above normal. 'The patient is the obsessional worrier — passive, sensitive, individualistic and highly strung,' wrote the psychologist. He continued with the following caution: 'He is also prone to be idealistic with literary and artistic interests.' And, once more, the graph line bounced highest in the area of sexuality: the masculine/feminine scale. The scandalous question of homosexuality raised its head again. In the psychologist's opinion, 'This patient is suffering severe conflict with his homosexual tendencies — the tension arising from his suppression of these unwanted desires causing emotional panic and acute anxiety reactions.'

There is no evidence that these findings were discussed with Brian, their implications teased out, or conclusions further tested. Instead, there is a brisk record of the exhaustive list of physical examinations conducted, none of which determined any problems — 'the blood levels of haemoglobin (91%), red cells normal; teeth excellent; abdomen – no tenderness; legs, feet, genitalia – N.A.D.' — before an equally brisk bureaucratic summary:

Diagnosis: Anxiety State
Assessment: Negligible
Fit for work
Copy of notes to be sent to L.M.O.

Brian returned to work. In October 1953, his 'L.M.O.' (local medical officer) referred him to a Dr Angus, whose cries of exasperation can be heard from half a century away. Brian, he noted: 'gives a history of attack of panic occurring from time to time, but these do not appear to be either of long duration or at all frequent. On the other hand he is very willing to discuss his various symptoms at great length and would not be averse to entering hospital for investigation. He is prepared, or so I think, to establish very quickly' — or, as Angus's secretary copies it in the typewritten version, in a Freudian slip that illuminates the patient's potential deviousness, 'very quietly' — 'a situation in which he would very rapidly become emotionally attached to, and extremely dependent upon, the therapy: this might accord well with Mr White's view that he has strong homosexual tendencies.'

Angus, it would appear, was of the old school. He summarised, with a brutality that Tom would have respected:

My feeling at the moment is that the ex-member [of the Armed Forces] —

    (a) should be kept out of hospital at all costs;

    (b) should be bullied into staying at work; and

    (c) should be kept well away from doctors for the present; at least should not be allowed to become dependent on the therapist.

However, Brian would or could not give up, as his symptoms bubbled up again and again to overwhelm the brittle shores of his resistance, and he pleaded with the local doctor for help.

In December, Angus was annoyed to discover that he had

unwittingly agreed to let Brian be readmitted to the hospital, following a telephone call from the country doctor during which Angus did not recollect Brian's name or the particulars of his case.

As soon as he recognised his mistake, Angus moved to have Brian discharged, commenting: 'admission to a psychiatric ward is likely to do him more harm than good'. Perhaps he was right, but it seems that Brian was unwilling, or unable, to be convinced.

Meanwhile, it was less than two months to his wedding.

Chapter Eleven

Brian and Joan's wedding, on Wednesday 10 February 1954, was a rather grand affair by Perth suburban standards. The reception was held at the Cottesloe Civic Centre, which sits among beautiful gardens and pine trees, atop a hill that tumbles down toward the sea.

I have the original proof sheet of the wedding photographs, given to me several years ago by Joan, soon after she was diagnosed with breast cancer. Being very healthy, never a smoker or a heavy drinker, she had been reading about breast cancer and its possible causes, wondering why, beyond the randomness of sheer bad luck, she may have been susceptible. She came across a theory that a trigger might be a repressed trauma of some kind, as if the shock waves of a terrible earlier event in one's life become trapped inside the body and go toxic.

This had made her think of Brian, his sudden death, how she had thought that the only way to cope, to protect her children, was to swallow the terrible story up inside herself, hold her breath, suffocate each and every runaway emotion as it was born. In asking the question, 'Why me?' of breast cancer, this was the only possible environmental factor that she could isolate, the only area of her life in which she felt she could, perhaps, have done something different to escape the disease.

Even if it wasn't truly the cause, it made her think. It made her want to summon up the courage to talk about Brian with her children.

Soon afterwards, I was passing through Adelaide, where she lived. She told me what she had been turning over in her mind. She gave me as many small pieces of her memory of Brian as she could provide, although mostly in the form of photographs rather than words, since the latter were harder to find and share.

The whole wedding unfolds, staccato-style, on the proof sheets. Joan's sister Marg and best friend Alison (who would later marry Eric), the two bridesmaids, with elegant winged collars and flowers in their hair, pose on the steps of the church, clutching their posies, their starched gowns sweeping out sideways in the wind in unison, as if tugged by unseen wires. Joan alights from the wedding car, gazing nervously at Alison and pulling at her own dress to keep it out of the dirt. She poses with her father, Jack, at the church door, steadying her composure, looking excited but faintly ridiculous under the delicate Coolgardie safe of the lace bridal veil. The next photo is the blooper that would never be circled for inclusion in the wedding album: father and bride are turning to enter the church just as a huge gust of wind billows her dress's tail up into a small tent in which the flower girls might happily play.

It was obviously deemed inappropriate to have the photographer popping flashbulbs during the religious ceremony, which is a notable elision in the visual record. But the wedding ritual at that time was standard enough that we can imagine how it must have proceeded. They didn't stray from the script or write their own.

Did any flickers of doubt about Brian's health cross the congregation as the ceremony proceeded? Do people fret about what may or may not go wrong in the future on a couple's wedding day? Surely not. Are not weddings, at their best, all about hope and affirmation?

Here's another shot: Joan and Brian take turns to sign the papers. She looks more relaxed now, with the veil cast off, pen in hand, as if about to confidently attack an exam paper. Meanwhile, refreshments are provided for some of the ladies in the church hall — the gents may have slipped outside to enjoy a cigarette or two.

As the couple joins the wedding party to pose for more formal photos outside the church, Brian's expression is hard to read: sometimes he smiles, but not always. Sometimes his mouth is set in a crease that hints at a kind of distance from the moment, as if he is a long way back inside himself, gazing out at what is happening. He laughs, but his joy is guarded. This may be his nerves or his natural reserve or, indeed, for that matter, entirely the projections of your narrator.

As the newlyweds bundle into the wedding car for the

reception, the guests mill around happily, grinning for the camera — the men in black tie, the younger women in floral-patterned long dresses, their elders in white fur stoles, hats, and elbow gloves.

At the dinner table at the Civic Centre, Tom sits next to Barbara, and Jack alongside Doris, all looking equally pleased with events. Brian's auntie Jess giggles and plays with a packet of cigarettes, while his younger brother Andrew Carlin beams with the flush of several beers.

There are speeches, of course, from the men: Tom, Jack, and Eric all take turns at the microphone, as does the priest, now seated, enjoying the company of an array of glasses of varying shapes and sizes. Brian, hands on hips, thanks the guests in reply. The assembled gathering make a toast, and the three-tiered cake is cut. Bride and groom take to the floor for the bridal waltz, with a dancing style that is less than flamboyant.

As the summer night deepens, they pose in a back room for one last set of photos, having changed now from formal wear into handsome street clothes for their honeymoon departure.

THE NEXT DAY, the newlyweds drove south for their beachside honeymoon, treading a well-known path to Caves House in Yallingup and on to a hotel in Margaret River. Within weeks, they were to discover that, despite taking 'certain precautions', Joan had fallen pregnant.

Joan joined Brian at Mount Barker, where he continued with his Agriculture Department posting. They rented a tiny cottage, 'a half-built house', half a mile out of town.

As the winter chill approached, at four months into the pregnancy, Joan lost the baby. She had few friends in the area, but her sister Marg came down to stay and comfort her.

Brian, the lone departmental officer at Mount Barker, reported to superiors in Albany, more than half an hour away by car. He drove for miles around the district, visiting farmers on their properties, often needing to stay overnight.

Joan strongly believed that travelling alone in the car didn't suit Brian's temperament. His only company, as the car snaked and slid across the gravel under the strobing sunlight of the gum trees, would have been his obsessive thoughts. *What is that pain in my left arm? And in my chest? Am I dying? Is it a heart attack? Why can I not stop these feelings? Are they real?* I watch the ideas flicker back and forth like shadows on his windscreen. The spiral into panic. Sometimes he is so afraid of what might happen that he finds himself stopping the car and turning back. *How can I explain this?* he says to the roadside bush, the magpies, and the sheep. He is humiliated by his weakness. And lying alone on a guest bed in a farmhouse with the Mackintosh sheet quietly spread across the bed, in case he pisses himself, his fear of death returns as he awakes, sweating in the moonlight. *The endless return, the endless circularity. How do others possibly face up to death? How can I live with this death inside me already?*

MEANWHILE, it was Tom, his father, dying. Cancer spreading from his bile duct.

In 1952, Tom had been posted to a command near the Montebello Islands in the north of Western Australia. He took charge of the Australian Army Forces stationed on guard on the mainland while the British conducted their nuclear test on the islands, in the top-secret Operation Hurricane.

I see him up there in his shorts and long socks, outside his tent in the desert camp, gazing resolutely towards the miraculous; the gorgeous billowing mushroom cloud in the tropical sky. He would have been right behind Prime Minister Menzies and his enthusiasm for the British mission: this was a power that the Empire needed to possess in the face of the communist threat and its Asian dominoes.

But, as he watched it, I imagine, he couldn't help but be impressed by the sheer beauty of the spectacle — never mind its strategic implications. The unfathomable force of that explosion expressed in the slow-motion dance of curling smoke. He would have liked to leap inside that cloud and feel its energy toss and turn him, lift him up like a waterspout on a whale. Someone once told me, or perhaps I dreamt, that Tom did indeed fly through the radioactive cloud of the Montebello test, in a light plane. Whether this was a monitoring flight, a sightseeing trip, or a mixture of the two, I'm not sure. The way I see it is like a scene from Kubrick's *Dr Strangelove*:

Tom flings open the window of the plane and inhales the poisonous air gleefully, hollering at the top of his voice. If he could, he'd surf these wild black waves, get inside that Nagasaki pipeline — Hiroshima, *mon amour*. Here he is, at the height of his powers! This is better than crawling across the brown dirt on a tractor on some wheat-belt farm. This is better than splashing through the Atlantic in an amphibious jeep. This is splitting the atom, cracking open the very stuff of the world and spilling it across the sky.

With Tom's very next breath, the cancer starts. It cosies up quietly, as usual, slipping in under his nose and biding its time. He doesn't know about it for a while. He comes back to Perth and doesn't talk about the bomb, having been sworn to the Official Secrets Act. He gets on with life.

Eric said Tom kept a regular appointment with his mates at the Scarborough pub after lunch on Saturday, coming home for dinner at 5.30 p.m. before falling asleep. On Sundays, the pubs were closed, but if he could arrange transport he'd make his way to drink at whichever army mess was open. He and Doris didn't go out together. They didn't have enough in common; she didn't drink, for a start.

As the excitement of the fireworks of Montebello fades, I imagine, the pain begins. Tom ignores it while he can, and consults a doctor when he must. The X-rays show the creeping shadow spread across his guts, and traces of it elsewhere. Already, it is too late. Suddenly, he is not only sick but dying. He is not good at dying, but grits his teeth as ever. He doesn't like to be pitied, so tells the blokes at the Scarborough front bar, the Masonic Lodge, the RSL, as little as possible. They have a beer and a fag together. He is barely in his fifties.

Tom went into hospital in 1954, and it was soon clear that he was not coming out *but in a box*. The family gathered at his bedside, Doris and their sons. Except for Brian. Brian was busy with his own problems in another wing of the hospital. Admitted to the psychiatric ward again.

Joan stayed, as usual, with Doris and Brian's younger brothers at Scarborough. Presumably, they all travelled to the hospital together sometimes for their various visits.

Tom was dying. Brian wasn't, although it appeared not for the first time that he might want to. He had made suicide attempts. No one knew how seriously to take them — weren't they always cries for help? Here in hospital, he had care second to none in the state. The psychiatrists kept up with the latest international trends and theories. This, to help them feel less like they were wandering completely in the dark.

Eric remembers that, on Tom's deathbed, he tried to reassure his father. 'Don't worry about anything at home.' It came out all wrong. 'Don't worry —' Tom withered him with his eyes. *What? Don't worry, I'm only dying?* To the last, he had this power, with just a look. *You don't measure up. None of you measure up.* Even behind the locked door of the psychiatric wing, Brian could hear him saying it.

Here I am blaming Tom again, just as my mother does. Tom, my cartoon villain. But I feel sorry for him, too, as his life finally slips away. He was born into a box, was he not? He merely grew to fill it.

Tom died, aged 52, on 13 August 1954, his family in the waiting room. Eric remembers the duty-sister asking whether they would like to view the body. 'No, thank you,' they said. Who wanted to look at death? Later, Eric found it surprising to see the open coffin at my mother's second partner Scott's funeral. 'He didn't look like a person — he looked like a statue or something.'

Which was true. His frozen face stretched upwards, as if gasping for a final breath. It was truly shocking, truly strange. It was no longer *him*. But maybe it helps to look at death's face, however strange and shocking, if the choice is the blank frame's haunting.

TOM'S FUNERAL. The women didn't go, of course; the women never went to funerals. They stayed at home with the curtains closed on their emotions. Joan and Alison sat with Doris at Abbett Street, drinking tea and listening to the ebbing time. The undertakers provided cards on which the mourner listed the family members that he represented. A hundred and fifty men filed along the paths of Karrakatta Cemetery and watched the coffin being lowered into the hole beneath the minister's brief words. Grim faces without eulogy or tears. Beers optional afterwards at a convenient *watering hole*. That was the sum of it.

Did they let Brian out to attend his father's funeral? This time, the psychologist had agreed that 'he should be thoroughly investigated'. Dr Angus was nowhere to be seen. Brian remained on the psychiatric ward for 16 weeks. A hospital social-behaviour chart mapped the trajectory of his stay, week by week. The chart is a litany:

He is never once 'rude' or 'profane' or 'domineering'.

He is not 'boastful', 'uncooperative', or 'irritable'.

He is not 'resentful', 'opinionated', 'argumentative', or 'sarcastic'.

He is neither 'mischievous' nor 'euphoric'.

He is not 'obstinate'.

He is never 'late for activities', and only twice is 'moderately' late for meals.

His room is never 'untidy'.

He is never 'ill at ease' with men or women, and only once does he 'avoid the opposite sex'. (This is the same disturbing week in early October in which he both engages in 'sexual talk' and is 'rejected by others'.)

Is he ever 'tearful', the chart asks? There is one week, early on, in which it is recorded, unusually, the words crammed into the tiny box meant for simple plus or minus signs, that he 'wants to be'. Interestingly, he never 'talks suicide'.

He regularly 'goes on weekend leave' to stay with Joan at Scarborough.

He is unfailingly 'well groomed', and 'cooperative' to routine.

Save for two weeks of flashpoint in October, leading to the time of 'sexual talk' when something trips him into paranoia and hallucinations, he is 'generally cheerful, socialises well', and makes 'appropriate conversation'. However, at the same time, he is consistently 'preoccupied', 'dependent on others', 'indecisive', 'anxious', 'tense', and 'depressed'.

He is 'restless'.

He is unceasingly 'self-centred', and 'talks excessively' about his illness.

And, as if manic, in the week leading up to the 'sexual talk' moment, he is markedly 'over-talkative' in general.

A NEW PSYCHIATRIST treating Brian suggested another radical therapy: full-coma insulin. Made popular by a neurophysiologist named Manfred Sakel in the 1930s, full-coma insulin was originally seen as another kind of shock therapy. It was another way that psychiatrists could feel that they were *doing* something.

Patients were injected with large doses of insulin, leading to profuse sweating, spasms, a slowing in breathing and, finally, a full coma, from which they would they be revived with glucose after 45 minutes or so. The procedure, administered without anaesthetic, was discomforting and dangerous, with up to 10 per cent of patients dying. Glucose, it was known, did not always succeed in awakening the patient. Assuming they did awake, they would have pissed, and often shat, themselves. As their speech and motor functions returned, they would be taken to the shower and cleaned up. After this, they ate voraciously. Their thoughts were slowed, their moods calmed.

Insulin therapy remained in vogue until studies began to appear in the late 1950s questioning its efficacy. New drugs worked better and were safer. Brian, in late 1954, was given 25 separate insulin treatments, amounting to a total of 16 hours of coma. This, the psychiatrist declared, left him 'greatly improved'.

BRIAN WAS EVENTUALLY DISCHARGED just before Christmas. He completed his rehabilitation with a working holiday on a friend's farm for six weeks over the summer.

Within the family and the department, discussions took place as to his future. It was agreed that a return to the isolation of Mount Barker was not advisable for his health. But, on the other hand, as his employer noted, 'he is keen upon fieldwork rather than office or laboratory activities'.

He didn't want to work in the city. He liked to be out on the ground with the farmers. An opening came up for a farm advisor on the northern wheat belt, in the Moora office. Brian took it.

My brother and sister were born in the Moora hospital; he in the summer of 1956, and she 18 months later.

Brian was happier in Moora, my mother remembers. The spells between his dark times lasted longer, and she could begin to hope that one day he might be free of them altogether.

What was the town like? My sister narrows her eyes as she tries to conjure up a vision: 'Flat and whitish. Dusty. A very boring asbestos house. A scrubby place.'

My brother swears that he remembers nothing, only photographs. There is a photograph of him as a baby held by Doris on the front step of the house; she must have come up on the bus to visit her first grandchild. This is how he knows what his house looked like.

But something he remembers, after all: the flood. The flood he saw one day from his bedroom window, the murky waters swirling ominously all around and underneath the house as if it were a boat adrift on the wide Amazon, or Noah's Ark on the day of God's wrath at Sunday school.

∽

I visit Moora, driving alone on a daytrip from Perth. I have no contacts there, no leads. Nobody in the family still has friends in the town. I go to have an image of the place, and in case there is a clue, a sign, a trace.

I drive in across the flatlands with the sun already low, the paddocks golden brown and fluttery. It is Sunday afternoon in town and the streets built wide seem even wider now with being empty. I cruise by the hospital: its familiar red-brick and tiles unchanged in 50 years. Majestic salmon gums tower above the rust-hued bitumen. Pubs are the grandest buildings of all — their fat, welcoming verandahs oozing around the corners of the major intersections. A stolid, squat brick building with a colonnaded portico announces itself twice. The words 'TOWN HALL' inscribed above its entrance find beneath them 'MOORA ROAD BOARD' written even larger, as if the business of local government had been once and forever subsumed under a single paramount task: fixing up the *bloody roads*.

I look for the house that our family lived in before I was born, on the main road into town. I find a row of such houses surviving intact from the '50s, embellished only with a scattering of iridescent plastic paddling pools. But, not knowing the number, I can't tell which was ours. I idly fantasise that an elderly person standing on a front lawn will recognise me, or rather recognise Brian in me, and flag me down to tell me stories of the old days. But there are no elderly people visible; they may as well have been washed away in the flood that my brother saw beyond his curtains.

It is hot enough still in April with the afternoon winding up. There's no point in staying longer, but I'm hungry before the long drive back to Perth. I get a hamburger at the Pioneer Bakery Tea Rooms, which looks — with its pool table out the back, its concrete floor, its plastic plants — like it might rev up with teenagers on a Friday night. But now, too early for dinner, too late for lunch, I'm the only customer.

☙

Brian was happier in Moora, my mother tells me. He liked the warmth; the dry air suited him. It may have reminded him of Kirk's Rock and his early childhood: the same bleached plains of stubble and gum, the wide-open spaces exuding calm.

He and Joan played golf and tennis with friends that they made through his work, from farms and the town. 'There was a good crowd there,' she remembers, 'a good crowd.' In the warm twilight after tennis, they could enjoy a drink and socialise. During the day, while Brian was off at work, Joan met up sometimes with the other wives who had babies of their own.

Brian was developing his career as a wheat and sheep advisor for the local cockies. He was young and energetic, up with all the latest scientific ideas. The more progressive of the district's farmers were open to the theories that he promoted about the stocking rates of sheep and the best way to encourage the good growth of clover in this harsh climate with its poor soils. Others were resistant; they didn't need any smart-alec city boy in a suit to tell them how to get their hands dirty. So he developed a strategy: concentrate on the few who were keen, and work with them intensely to devise and conduct trials on their farms; then, organise field days and invite all the other farmers to see for themselves the results.

Lines of utes came crawling across paddocks to park in long rows beside a fence or track, and the farmers in their hats assembled to hear Brian proselytising from the back of a truck. They were surprised to find how much they liked him. He had a way of explaining things that they could relate to: not too fancy, not *with a bloody test tube stuck up his arse*. He charmed them with a few good jokes. They would all help themselves to morning tea, and poke around in the paddock a bit to see for themselves whatever evidence there may be in the pasture growth, or the health of the sheep, to support his claims. They would mutter and squint and shove their hands deeper in their pockets and, afterwards, as the first of the utes were backing out and kicking up dust as they turned onto the gravel, a few of the cockies would linger and quietly approach Brian. He'd get out his diary and make appointments to come and visit them, and they'd agree to take it from there. *He's a good bloke, that Brian Carlin. He's got his head screwed on.*

But even in Moora, the screws came loose sometimes.

Sometimes Brian felt an overwhelming need to talk to Eric. He would call him up and they would arrange to meet at a pub, and Eric would know that Brian was in trouble by the tone of his voice across the wire, no longer that of the big brother demonstrating the technological marvels of the tin can in the Mandurah sanddunes. This was the brother who had already shown the capacity to do more than contemplate suicide. There was desperation and urgency in that voice: *You must come, I have to talk.*

Face to face in the pub, with only the necessary travelling time having elapsed, they would order a beer. And — ? Perhaps Brian would stammer or cough or trace his beer across its watery curves on the bar. Perhaps he was ashamed and couldn't find any words that would make sense to his brother, just blown in from some happy world and looking to him as if to say, *Let's sort this out before the next round of beers*. Perhaps he felt better just to be there, close and familiar and looking back at the ridiculousness of the panic that drove him to the telephone.

Eric would wait; Brian would say nothing. They would make small talk about the weather and the footy. Eric didn't ask because he didn't know how to ask, or even what to ask about. Besides, he didn't want there to be anything to ask about. So both of them would wait, and Brian wouldn't say, because … But we are going around in circles. Eric would order another round of beers, bemused to be called out all this way for nothing, but perhaps relieved not to have been invited in to Brian's black imaginings.

Once, Brian called up from Moora. Eric, in Perth at the time, gathered together a weekend bag, and drove with Alison through the hours of a moonlit Friday evening towards the lights of the sleepy town.

Brian and Eric went to the pub, leaving Joan and Alison at home where the babies slept. Of course, when the brothers sat down at the pub with their beers, as if in a folktale, the same thing happened: only small talk in the smoky air between them.

BRIAN WAS EMOTIONALLY DEMANDING. This is a recurring theme in all the people I talk to — apart from Joan. She will not say a word against him. She prefers to turn attention to her own faults: 'I wasn't a good listener for him.'

He, for his part, according to what he told the doctors over the years, as recorded in scattered notes, thought she was too good for him. He was unclean, impure; she on a pedestal. Shame is scattered like a condiment across this story.

One time — I'm not sure when — one of Brian's best friends from university, David Fischer, took him up to see the view from the roof of the freshly completed tallest building in Perth, above the head offices of the bank where he worked.

Brian was out on weekend leave from the hospital and, with Joan and the kids in the country, he was staying with David and his wife. As they walked around the rooftop, David joked: 'Now don't do anything silly like jumping off.'

Chapter Twelve

Was Brian born into the wrong time? Would things be different for him now? Would the new medications, cognitive therapies, save him? Sometimes it seems he was that close to surviving, to discovering how to get out of the sheep tracks in his brain.

According to neuroscientists, we all wear neuronal grooves in our brains as familiar thought associations flow from A to B to C. For those in mental trouble, like Brian, the sheep tracks are negative, destructive ones: deep gutters of despair eroding away the healthy topsoil. I am determined to pursue this clumsy agricultural metaphor, because this is the way I would explain it to Brian: *It's like your brain is a paddock, Dad — and, by the way, have you noticed that your name is only a slip of the typing fingers away from being 'Brain', which is kind of ironic, don't you think? Anyway, think of your brain as a paddock with these sheep tracks, and you can actually find new ways to get across the paddock. You can retrain those sheep, which are your thoughts, remember, to climb out of their well-worn paths and walk in different directions, from A to H and back to A again, so then they say 'Aha!' in sheep language. And you would feel happier, that's the point.*

Brian was famous throughout the West Australian countryside for his work with sheep and paddocks, so this is why he would be receptive to this metaphor. What he put into widespread practice for the first time was the simple-sounding idea that you could maintain a lot more sheep than previously thought in any given paddock, because their feeding would stimulate the clover to grow better and provide more feed; and hence you could create a virtuous circle of productivity, unlike the vicious circles of negative thoughts that he might experience in the car to and from the field days.

This new theory was called 'set stocking', and it replaced the conventional wisdom, called 'rotational stocking', which held that you rotated the sheep back and forth between paddocks and did not have too many in any one area at a time.

The theory was based on the latest scientific understanding about pastures, including such things as subterranean clovers, which boffins at the Commonwealth Scientific and Industrial Research Organisation had proved in trials at field stations, but which Brian took and demonstrated, like a magic trick, in a real farmer's paddock. This was a way to make the land more productive, and farming more profitable.

Whether the new methods were environmentally sustainable in the long run is another matter. It sounds bad — all those trampling cloven hooves pounding on the subterranean clover, those sideways-chewing sheep mouths gobbling it up as soon as it surfaced.

But Brian held it wasn't like that at all; in fact, it was like going back to nature. He wrote in articles that kangaroos have their particular places where they like to eat, and it's the same with sheep.

∾

Listen to me now, Brian. Jim Frith, another of your friends from Agriculture at university who became a farmer for a time, last saw you walking across the main street of Bridgetown a few days before you died, 'big smile' on your face, 'up straight and everything, happy as Larry', and you were off 'on a field trip to put in some plots somewhere'; you had 'a program of sowing plots of clover and oats, and so on'. You were so cheery, 'bright and breezy', and he thought, 'Thank God, that's over!' Because, the previous week, he had experienced a strange episode with you in the Land Rover on his farm, in which the two of you were out inspecting this and that, and drove to the top of a hill in the bush, and you stopped the car and started to talk. You talked about your old lecturer and friend Henry Schapper, and how he had been pointing you out at gatherings and saying derogatory things about you; how very, very bad you were, and how good Joan was, 'the pinnacle of rectitude and beauty'. Henry, to your mind, was an 'evil genius' who had found you out.

You talked on and on for an hour, an hour and a half and, because Jim was younger then and not so experienced in the world, he didn't know what was going on, what to do or say. At first, he took everything you said seriously, the penny only dropping slowly that 'you were out of your bloody mind'. You were saying things to do with sex: you thought the very act was unclean; you were a perpetrator, just as your father seemed to be when you heard him through the hessian wall and saw what he was doing to your mother.

Brian! This is your analyst speaking now. Tell me, was this the scene that retrospectively shocked your childhood mind, which knew nothing of female anatomy and presumed an anal penetration just like the ones you later suffered on the jetty from the American kitchenhands? Let's pretend that it's a séance and you can move the glass to indicate 'yes' or 'no'.

After the scene in the Land Rover, and after Brian's suicide the following week, Jim felt like an idiot for not offering more help. But in between the two events, he saw him cross the road that day so 'bright and breezy'. In his grief and confusion, he went to speak to Henry, who told him for the first time the story about Brian's gang rape.

JIM IS A MAVERICK. In his old age, he has spent a decade, alongside his wife, Mary, campaigning for the local native forests. In the old days, he used to roll cigarettes with his hands below the steering wheel, driving at dusk along gravel roads. He still likes a glass of red and a good story. Out in the jarrah gazebo at the corner of their farmhouse, he talks to me for hours about Brian.

This sheep track: *the unclean, the impure, the purity of others.* Up there on the hill, as Jim remembers it, Brian 'had this feeling of behavioural inferiority somehow'. Coupled with 'this sense of duty'. Which, in the end, became the duty, as he saw it, to kill himself. To which, I think, would not the repression of some homosexual feelings explain all this?

Jim says: 'No, I think I can say this quite clearly. My daughter is homosexual and I'm not embarrassed by it. I never had any thought that he might have been homosexual. No. He just had these — this sense of duty ...'

This is interesting, because Jim, out of all my father's friends and relations, would be the one least invested in protecting Brian (or myself, or the family at large) from the supposed slur of *batting for the other team*. I find his testimony convincing. It seems that Brian's psychic reality was more mixed up and complex, his problems deeper than could have been resolved with a simple coming out.

BUT I AM GETTING AHEAD OF MYSELF again. Brian, before the last days in Bridgetown, was living and working in Moora. He stayed out of hospital for over four-and-a-half years. He saw an innovative young psychiatrist, a Dr Derham, who, among other things, prescribed Largactil, a brand of the new anti-anxiety, anti-psychotic drug chlorpromazine that remains commonly prescribed today. Derham recommended that Brian increase the dosage of Largactil at times of stress, to such a point that in 1956 the local doctor in Moora received a letter from the Repatriation Commission querying his prescription of 1000 tablets in less than four months.

After this, for three years, there is not even a whisper in the medical records. These were the good times. Joan could relax a little from the constant fear of his next relapse.

BRIAN WAS DOING SO WELL at his job that the department decided he was needed elsewhere to bring his energy and ideas to the conservative old-school areas of the deep south-west, where farming dynasties a century old had established their own very comfortable sheep tracks.

In 1960, Brian and Joan moved the family to Bridgetown. Joan speaks of it now as if she had a premonition that this would be bad for Brian: the chill in the air, the fogs cotton-wooling the river valleys. Would it be a return to their early days and the mists of Mount Barker that her new husband so quickly dissolved in?

They rented a little green weatherboard cottage in a back street of Bridgetown. I glean the details from my siblings, the memories of small children.

My sister, Wendy, didn't like the house being made of wood. She worried it would burn down. There were always bushfires in the summer. Once, Brian drove the family right through a bushfire in the Falcon station wagon, looking for a picnic spot. The countryside was black and smouldering, and Joan was upset that he wouldn't turn around. After he died and Joan moved us all to Perth, Wendy was relieved that the new house was made of brick.

At the front of the house in Bridgetown was a verandah with tea chests and boxes full of clothes for dress-ups. Inside, a lounge room faced the street. Here, the new stereo would come to have pride of place, with its inbuilt speakers at either end, and the turntable in the cabinet in the middle, on which Brian played show-tunes from *Camelot, The King and I*, and *Oklahoma!*, and sometimes Peter, Paul, and Mary. On the night Brian didn't come home, my brother, John, remembers Mum playing records on that stereo. John knew something wasn't right, even though she reminded him that 'sometimes he does stay out overnight'. That was true, but usually he would call to let them know. In the silence, to ease the tension, she played records, as Brian would have done.

Wendy and John shared a bedroom, their beds parallel. When I came along, I slept those few months in a cot in my parents' bedroom. The kitchen, the hub of life, lay at the rear. On top of the fridge stood Brian's boxes of cigarettes. Wendy knew that smoking was bad, and later surmised that this could have been what killed him.

Beyond the kitchen window lay the back garden. There was a grassy area by the back door, one large tree, and a woodheap at the rear where Brian chopped wood. Once, he accidentally struck his finger with the axe. John and Wendy saw it bleeding. It was the worst thing that they ever saw happen to him.

The McKinnons, who lived next door with three or four older kids, set up a high jump in their backyard. One day, one of the girls misjudged her leap and skewered her sister's leg with the bamboo stake that served as the high-jump bar. Blood gushed everywhere, much more so than from Brian's finger. They rushed the poor girl to the hospital. It was just like when Brian's brother Andrew fell out of the tree and skewered his skull on the picket fence, or when our neighbour Katy Brown got hit by a car crossing the Esplanade in Perth in the bucketing rain, on her way to watch a travelling circus. Childhood is full of such abrupt disasters.

Barry McKinnon, who later entered Parliament, was a notorious tearaway. He used to lead John across into the paddocks at the end of the street to the seclusion of a little shed, where he would exhibit contraband: a cigarette or two. In those days, you could wander around the neighbourhood at will until your mum called you from the front step to come home for tea.

I HAVE TO REMIND MYSELF that this picture of life in Bridgetown includes me in a last-reel cameo. I have to make an effort to insert myself into the frame. The movie version would have me represented by a swaddled doll of some kind, viewed indirectly, with baby sounds subtly inserted on the soundtrack. It seems that my arrival became so mixed up with Brian's death not long afterwards that there are no specific memories to speak of. Or perhaps I haven't asked to hear them? I have no idea of the details of my birth, or the role Brian played in the event. I have a photograph of Brian holding a small baby at a beach, but the baby is my brother, John, playing a stand-in for my role. Just as Brian later vanished, I as an infant recede from view.

∾

I wondered if Brian talked to Joan a lot about his work, if she helped him out, given it was her field, too. But she said that she kept pretty well out of it. It was his business; that's how they saw it. She was occupied with the kids, helping out at the kindergarten, making clothes to sell at the fête. Indeed, she believed at the time that her university degree in Agriculture had been perfectly useless to her.

At Bridgetown, Brian began again with organising field days, sending out feelers to whichever farmers might be open to new ideas. If the old blokes were too stuck in their ways, he'd start up conversations with their sons and plant his foot in the door that way. He'd say: 'For God's sake, get your worst paddock and try two sheep to the acre, and compare the pasture to what your old man does with his one sheep. And if that works, try three sheep, and so on.'

He met up with one young bloke called Bert Read, who had a few hundred acres just outside of Bridgetown. Bert and Jim Frith became Brian's greatest local supporters. They took turns to be presidents of the new Farm Management Club, set up by Henry Schapper with Brian's help, in which farmers were encouraged to keep track of all their facts and figures on paper, so they could manage their sheep and crops and fertilisers and everything else scientifically, and not just by following whatever their fathers or their neighbours had happened to do in the past.

Bert loved any sort of new ideas, and he liked the way Brian thought. One time, he decided to get into producing fat lambs. He'd traipsed after Brian, down to Rocky Gully, near Mount Barker, where new land had been opened up under the Soldier Settlement scheme.

Bert asked out loud how it was that these ex-servicemen,

living in tents and with no previous farming experience, were producing such beautiful fat lambs? To which Brian replied, deadpan: 'Well, Bert, they don't have any farmers to hold them back.'

Brian didn't mess around. He told the farmers what was what. Bert remembers a field day over in Boyup Brook, Brian telling the audience of hats: 'Don't clear all your land, just do strips. Clear less land but fertilise it; put on four bags of super and you'll get results now, good clover.' Bert was impressed: the standard advice was that you had to wait four to five years for that.

The old blokes spat into the dust and said, 'What would the bloody Ag. Department know?' But the bank manager on the main street of Bridgetown told Bert's wife, Gwen, in private, that Bert was by far the best farmer in the district.

Brian ran quite a few of his field days up at Bert's place, where 30 to 100 farmers would come to hear him talk. He cut a striking figure up there on the ute: one part military leader marshalling his troops, and one part spiritual guide converting the masses to a new path for salvation.

Even Tom would have been proud of him on field days, surely — although he wouldn't have said it. He would have found something to criticise. A certain withering intellectual pride runs in the family. If a farmer asked a silly question, like, 'Why is that cow fatter than that other cow?' Brian would say, 'Probably eats more.'

He wasn't without his enemies. A man called Farley from out Boyup Brook way wrote letters to the local paper. He lived in an area where clover grew like a weed, and he couldn't see the point in Brian's theories on high stocking rates, regarding them as arrogant and dangerous, and saying as much in his series of published letters.

Jim Frith thought Brian was more sensitive to this type of criticism than did him good. But Bert said: 'Brian was always positive with us. Once or twice, with a cup of tea, he might mention he had a headache.'

Because these things were hidden. Brian kept up appearances until the last possible moment each time his symptoms worsened. And Joan never spoke to a single soul about Brian's illness. Not even with her closest friends did she feel able to confide. The less said the better, all agreed, *without saying it.*

And perhaps I didn't mention this? Within the first month of arriving in Bridgetown in 1960, before he had hardly started working with Bert Read, Brian was in trouble and spending time back in hospital in Perth.

Recommending his admission, Dr Derham had described him as 'severely depressed and obsessed with pessimistic ideas'. Once in hospital, Derham conducted extensive psychotherapy sessions with Brian. On 11 August 1960, he wrote in Brian's case sheet:

[The patient is] worried, very slow in speech and movement, preoccupied with psychic conflict and rumination about mental mechanisms, which he discusses at a tedious pace. As ever, there is much intellectualisation, and a considerable amount of sophistication.

Mr Carlin consciously aims towards insight and adjustment.

He gives a reasonable account of recent happenings in his life in a general way, indicating a steady decline in his work and increasing depression during the past month. Loss of libido during the past three months he relates to his 'high MF' [the high score on the masculine/feminine scale on the MMPI psychological test]; he repeatedly castigates himself for marrying, believing that his wife would be better without him (Mrs Carlin tends to blame herself for his present condition, having encouraged him to do postgraduate study this year).

Derham prescribed Largactil three times a day, plus the barbiturate sodium amytal at night, but now added injections of intramuscular Tofranil four times daily. The latter was the first of the tricyclic anti-depressants, which appeared a generation before the Selective Serotonin Reuptake Inhibitors (SSRIs), of which Prozac is most famous.

Within a week, Derham noted an improvement, and by the end of the month thought it an excellent sign that Brian had taken it upon himself to make a stepladder in the hospital workshop. He continued, in his notes:

Progressing ... His obsessive rumination still includes topics of dying, self-destruction, self-criticism, hetero and homosexuality, cowardliness, etc, but the lifting of mood is continuing and with it increased activity, sociability and productiveness. Reduction of night sedation is suggested with continued oral Tofranil.

By this point, Derham could run through the roll of Brian's pet obsessions like a shopping list of everyday poisons.

BRIAN'S MIND: a sorcerer's maze of shifting walls and mirrors in which he finds himself forever consigned to wander, searching in vain for an exit, finding only familiar cul de sacs, tricky loops, ornate spirals. A landscape endlessly, morbidly fascinating and depressing, because it is the territory he knows best, the place he returns to over and over in an attempt to solve the riddle trapping him. He cannot see that the walls he scrapes his thoughts against are hollow, flimsy things, no more than oxygen and electricity coursing through his skull.

To the outsider, to his friends and family, to Joan, to the doctors: they watch him, in the deep dullness of his eyes, gathering all his strength to swat imagined flies, flinch at non-existent blows, endure the pounding of his own merciless attacks. They watch his exhausting dance of death, but he is too distant, across a wide river of unreason and absurdity, for them to reach him.

He knows he must not speak, must not call out, because once he starts he will descend once more into the maze, and they will look at him bemused and pained, and he will be spreading to them the toxins he has gathered. This resolve not to call out any longer becomes the will to suicide.

I have visited that maze myself, or something similar, in my own disputes with depression. But I am not Brian, I know that now. I have never been to where he went. Do I sound harsh towards him? I would like to be *his* father, to look after him, to wrap him in my arms as my child. To teach him consolation. It was not as if he didn't try; this much is clear. It seems he pushed all his adult life to extract himself but, like a bogged car spinning its wheels, only wound his way in deeper.

BRIAN SPENT FIVE WEEKS IN HOSPITAL in August and September 1960, and a further six or seven weeks working for the Department of Agriculture in Perth, while Joan and the children stayed with Doris in Scarborough.

In November, the doctors deemed him fit to return to his normal job in Bridgetown.

Derham asked Brian to visit him every month or so to check upon his progress. In February, Derham commented: 'He is as ever working towards greater insight.' By this time, Derham believed that the doses of Tofranil and Largactil could be tapered off, and gave Brian licence to temporarily increase the Tofranil from time to time should he feel depressive symptoms rising.

The psychic truce in Brian's mind lasted eight months. He resumed his field work with Bert Read and others, including Joan's father, Jack, who was keen to try out Brian's ideas on the family farm at Kojonup, 150kms to the east of Bridgetown.

But in June 1961, the darkness struck again: this time, he was deeply depressed and suicidal. Who knows what precipitated each cycle of collapse? Joan says there was no warning. He apparently had a remarkable ability to shield her and the world at large from his true thoughts and feelings.

Derham booked him straight back into Hollywood Hospital, and instructed that he be closely watched for suicide attempts.

'Very depressed and stating he will take his life,' commented one nurse. 'Continually wanting attention,' added another the same day. That night, he slept soundly, but in the morning was missing from the ward and found wandering in the gardeners' workshops. 'Keep under close observation,' reiterated the nurse. The patient's mood was not improving.

Derham prescribed activity, participation, and Tofranil by intramuscular injection. Hospital staff were directed to interest Brian in bridge games in the evenings. Derham persuaded him to attend occupational therapy again, where they were doing leatherwork. 'Please keep [him] fully occupied,' he instructed. Brian needed distraction from his destructive obsessional thoughts. He told Derham that he had attempted to hang himself with his dressing-gown cord, because he believed it was the right and honest thing to do and it would bring greater disgrace upon his children and his family if he dithered and was too cowardly to proceed.

Derham, of all the doctors, was the one who took the time to get closest to recording Brian's voice. He had the patience, empathy, or professional curiosity to note the relentless twists and turns of Brian's obsessions: 'He feels he is only half a man and should not have married ... [believes] staff in the faculty thought he had been here three weeks and should be condemned for lacking the courage to kill himself ...'

Derham increased the dosage of the Tofranil injections and, for the first time in ten years for Brian, recommended ECT. He urged caution, since Brian recalled benefiting from the first two previous treatments but panicking after the fourth. This time, however, the response appeared positive, with an immediate lift in mood and an ability to gain a healthier perspective on his obsessive thoughts.

After several weeks, he was released from hospital once more, and returned to Bridgetown to take up where he left off.

NOW IT WAS ONLY SIX WEEKS before the call came. Brian had swallowed an overdose of sodium amytal capsules, Derham recorded, 'after meditating in a dilemma about people in the district discussing his "lack of courage to do one thing or the other".' There was, again, no warning. His work performance had been normal.

The local Bridgetown doctor performed a stomach pump, and Brian stayed overnight in hospital in Bridgetown before Joan drove him up to Perth to see Derham. The children were billeted with friends.

ON HIS WAY TO PERTH, my Brian already feels better, as if making the attempt itself has been a temporary relief. It is a sign of courage, is it not, attempting suicide? Now they can't criticise him for inaction. He has proved his manliness, for Tom and Uncle Ben, and Grandpa Carlin, and all the blokes whom he knows, or whom he sees buying drinks at the pub and doesn't know at all, who seem to share their hard-set jaw, their sneer, their untroubled *masculinity*. To rise above his weakness, to be redeemed in their imagined eyes, he must destroy the enemy — himself. Thus his thoughts flicker past with the white mileposts by the highway edge.

Joan drives the car. How to imagine the constant stress she must feel as each day threatens to yield a new collapse, fresh horror? What would he choose next? Would she find him dead, or merely missing, waiting for someone else to find him? The man she has married, the man she has chosen to spend her life with, the man whose children she is raising: no matter what she does, she cannot find a way inside to help him. It makes no sense, any of it. He wants for nothing. He is successful and well loved. Why can he not be happy? Why can he not disentangle himself from the thoughts that choke him? She is young. Her mind doesn't work the way his seems to. She cannot fathom it. She continues day to day as best she can. She wishes it could be over *but not in that way*. She should be able to save him. Her love should be enough to save him.

He knows that, too. He knows that her love should be enough to save him. He knows that all he has should be enough. He is logical and knows this to be true. Hence, since it is evidently not enough, as he proves time and again when the depression drowns him, it follows *logically* that the fault lies within himself. *There is no reason for anything to be wrong with me, yet something is wrong with me: hence, the reason lies within me, and I myself am what is wrong. I have tried and tried to think it through and come out the other side, but the more I think it through the more — but you know about my maze, you have already been discussing it.* (You see how he, Brian — how easily he slips inside the narrator's cloak?)

Chapter Thirteen

It is true, Dr Derham, that I have been observing people talking about me again, suggesting if I had the courage I would end it all. Last week, I even heard someone say this while I was mowing the lawn and quite alone. Now that is surely madness, is it not, Dr Derham?

It is November now and, although for a while I was too busy to worry, lately these thoughts have been marshalling their forces, shall we say. Yes, morbid ideas, as you call them. Now we come into your office and my wife bursts into tears. You see the suffering I am causing her? I will go back to the hospital, I will be safe there, perhaps. I will sign a consent form for you to connect up the electrodes to my head again — although I don't recall having to do so earlier; perhaps this is a new regulation that has come in?

The hospital is so familiar now; it is where my other self belongs. I put on my pyjamas and trudge around among the mad, the shell-shock victims, the blokes who never came back from the war. What of my war? The jetty. Drunk in Little Lonsdale, the door we opened. What she gave me. Pissing razorblades. Sex is a kind of cruelty. Why do people have to be so dirty? Why couldn't you put your dirty filthy shaving brush away, Father, instead of leaving it dripping in the bathroom? I shake it in your face, but I am not strong enough to withstand the cyclone of your fury. Don't tell me what to do in my own house! *But is there something wrong with wanting things to be clean?*

Am I talking too fast?

Sometimes, I talk too slowly with Dr Derham. My thoughts are distant, and it takes a lot of time and effort to retrieve them. He is very patient. He makes an effort to understand me. He might be able to solve the case, if I can only give him enough clues. He respects my intelligence. He can see I'm not an idiot. Jack Neale did say to me in Moora, Why don't you just bloody do it instead of talking about it all the time? *It's not like I'm making it all up. People say these things all the time. They might be joking, but behind every joke there's a grain of truth. We used to talk about that in psychology. A joke is like having something both ways.*

Schapper is another one. He's a smart bloke. He was like a brother to me at the hostel the night the thunderstorm came and I fell out of bed. He was in the next-door room. I could talk to him then. I told him about the jetty. But I know what he thinks now.

What is the ECT doing to my head? It's hard to remember things sometimes. Sometimes I have it every morning.

But often I am not in the hospital. It is like a nightmare I wake up from. In fact, I can travel the whole of 1962 and most of 1963 without visiting the hospital. In Bridgetown, I go to Apex Club meetings. I build things for the playground at the kinder working bee. I go on picnics with Joan and the kids, and I taste the water in the creek where we stop for lunch to see if it is fit to drink. My kids look at me and see a very tall father. Joan and I have a discussion group with Bert and Gwen Read and Jim and Mary Frith that we organise through Adult Education. They send us books, and we meet once a month and take it in turns to give little talks. Gwen gives one on music.

If I forget to take my Tofranil at lunchtime out on the road, working, Derham says, that's what brings the symptoms back.

DERHAM WROTE, upon seeing Brian on 12 August 1963:

Very satisfactory. He is cheerful, working as ever, and has negotiated the birth of his third child without mishap. No mention was made of his symptoms today. Tofranil continued at present level — 50mg.q.i.d. Review in seven weeks recommended (Appointment 10.15am, 30.9.63)

On 29 September, Brian, Joan, and family drove to Perth to stay overnight at Doris's before his appointment.

Next morning, a Monday, at 8.30 a.m. he set off from Scarborough for Derham's rooms. He never came home that day or night.

At 7.15 a.m. on Tuesday, Joan phoned Derham to ask what had happened when he saw Brian the previous day. Derham confirmed her fears: Brian never showed up for his appointment.

She had already called the police, having spent another sleepless night waiting for him. She had got the children up and pretended nothing was wrong. She had shown Doris that she was not too worried, so Doris would not be worried, and Doris tried to do the same in return. It was a domestic chamber masquerade, although Doris had trouble staying in her role.

At 11.30 a.m., Joan called Derham again to say that Brian had arrived home at last, staggering through the back door in a kind of daze with, as Derham understood it, 'little recollection of his actions over much of the past 24 hours'. The police called off their search. Joan drove Brian straight to Derham's rooms. On the way, and upon arrival, Brian was restless and agitated.

'I haven't slept,' he said to Derham, although perhaps you will excuse me if I embellish (again) the exact details of his conversation, since Derham's notes, which are all I have, can never be exhaustive. A monologue for Brian, addressing Derham:

I didn't come to see you. But of course you know that. It was enough to spend the evening in my father's house again. I decided — I don't know when it was I thought of it — I took all the Tofranil I had. I swallowed it in the car shortly after I left home. I pulled over by the beach. Maybe 50 or 60 tablets. It's supposed to make you feel better if you take enough; you just take more if you feel the need, that's what you told me. Fifty or 60 was not a number I had tried before.

I decided to drive north of town to Burns Beach, where it would be quiet and I could be alone to do what I had to do. But how? What is the best way to destroy what you need to destroy?

I'm not sure if I wandered into the ocean. I took off my trousers at one point. I know that because later I wasn't wearing them.

Later, I was looking for wildflowers in the bush, in the sand dunes. I know the botanical names of many wildflowers. It is the wildflower season: spring. I had to get away from people. My legs and feet were scratched, my face, too; I must have scraped it on something. Maybe I scraped it on the sand under the water as I drowned. Except I didn't drown, or I wouldn't be here looking at you again, Dr Derham.

I'm not sure if you do have any answers, Dr Derham, do you?

You know the worst thing? The mosquitoes. They ripped into me. They obviously don't mind a bit of Tofranil. I couldn't find my clothes or briefcase, I'm not sure where I left them. But I found the car, eventually. I came across it and I thought: There it is! But of course it was locked, and I didn't have the key, because it was in my trousers.

Luckily, another car was there by now, in the car park, and a man, who helped me break into the Falcon and get it going. He asked if I was alright and I said I was not too good, I'd had a bad night but I was going home now. I think he thought I'd had a big night on the grog. I didn't want him to worry, just to help me with the car.

Only he said all this more mumbled and be-drugged and stuttery, and with long gaps in which he just breathed and stared back into the night.

Derham listened, and afterwards wrote a note quiet in its drama: 'The question of leucotomy arises as the surest treatment to prevent similar relapses. I would appreciate Dr Zeck's opinion on this case.'

So, for the first time, Derham seriously contemplated the efficacy of corrective brain surgery for Brian. Perhaps it was only now that Brian's case had reached such a point of crisis; perhaps Derham had been reading in the literature of new successes with lobotomy in similar cases. Certainly, he was getting desperate, as Brian's desire and capacity for effective suicide apparently grew stronger despite all the treatments tried.

Joan was a mess. To put on a brave face was an effort akin to climbing at high altitude without oxygen. She drove Brian home to Scarborough to pack him a bag, and then took him in to Hollywood Hospital, where he was admitted by 4.00 p.m.

Who knew how long he would remain there this time?

Wendy and John, in their first and second year of school respectively, would have to attend the nearest primary school in Scarborough for the duration. Joan would drive back to Bridgetown, with the baby in a bassinet on the front seat, to bring up more clothes and their satchels; she had been expecting to stay only two nights. Doris would take the kids up to the grocers to buy supplies and a lolly.

Brian's arrival in hospital coincided with a holiday that Derham had planned. In Derham's absence, Dr Zeck assumed the lead role in Brian's care. Without a history with Brian, Zeck seemed less inclined to empathise:

> Seen briefly (files not to hand). He seems to present a picture of a pseudoneurotic schizophrenia at present. There is much … posturing and gesticulation — I am not sure if this may be a hangover from his Tofranil intake. See again next week.

No doubt Zeck had many other patients; he was busy, tired. He might have been preoccupied with his golf handicap.

He might not fit my stereotype at all. I have irrationally taken against him mostly because he shows no interest in performing magic on Brian. I believe by this time a shaman or a Buddhist monk might have been of more assistance. And, needless to say, it was grossly unfair of Derham to have gone on holiday just when Brian needed him.

However, with the benefit of sleep and significant doses of Largactil, Brian calmed again, and within a day or so the nurses reported that he was bright and sociable and much improved. On the fourth day, one commented cheerily that he 'would have played tennis today but no sandshoes to fit him'.

Joan came in to visit Brian with the children. Wendy remembers him wearing a maroon-checked dressing gown and slippers. He would have made an effort to look debonair even there. Tall, with the afternoon light streaming in, he might almost have been in a smoking jacket, inviting friends in for a civilised pre-dinner drink.

Noel brought Doris in one day. 'I could never work out what the bloody hell was going on,' Noel told me, 'I never saw a single sign of mental illness.' Which tells as much about Noel's acuity as it does about Brian's social skills, but nevertheless ...

On weekend leave, Brian said to Noel out of the blue (everything came to Noel out of the blue): 'Come on, we're going for a drive.' He took him up to Burns Beach to the very spot where he'd previously parked the car.

The scene in broad, fresh daylight was peaceful, even banal. The prickly scrub hovered in a horizontal mat above the sand. Scraps of rubbish ejected from car windows lay below.

They hunted around in the bush, and Brian was able to locate everything he had lost: his wristwatch, wallet, and loose change. 'We found it all except for a few coins,' said Noel. 'It was as if we were going to the footy or something. Took me a while to get over that trip.'

A week later, on 10 October, Zeck's diagnosis had solidified: 'It seems quite definite that [Brian] felt that "everybody" felt it would be best for him to commit suicide. I feel that this is a paranoid projection in a delusional system.' *Whack!* Take that, Brian! 'There is other supporting evidence of a similar nature which in my mind confirms the diagnosis of schizophrenia.'

It is unclear whether he shared these conclusions with his patient.

SCHIZOPHRENIA? At this late stage, can we accommodate yet another name to contain Brian's problems? After so many years with depression, obsessional neurosis, anxiety condition, and the rest? And isn't schizophrenia of an entirely different nature?

I sent a copy of Brian's medical records to Dr Hugh Cook, our former GP turned psychiatrist who had helped Wendy all those years ago and facilitated the revelatory conversation with my mother. I wanted to see how he would interpret the records from the standpoint of a contemporary professional in the field; what light he could shed on Brian's illness and the treatments offered him.

Hugh Cook was semi-retired by then. He lived with his wife in a simple but beautiful apartment with a wall of glass looking directly onto the Swan River in Claremont.

He offered me a cup of tea, and we joined up some of the dots between our families. One of his daughters is an old friend of my sister ... one of his sons, who had gone to high school with me, is now himself a school principal ... and so on.

And Brian, the records? Hugh talked very quietly, in measured tones. He had known Derham: 'Somewhat irascible, highly intelligent.' Maybe he was even still alive; he had been until recently. 'He had an excellent memory, was the kind of guy who would remember every detail of every one of his patients.'

I imagined myself listening to Brian's chief psychiatrist remember every detail from 40 years prior. This would be the closest I would ever come to meeting Brian in his raw, openly ill condition. There might be conclusions, insights, that Derham could formulate, beyond those scratched in his terrible handwriting. It might be he who held the key to finally unlock the mystery. I knew quite well that there almost certainly was no key, but still, but still — this 'but still' is what I believe old Sigmund F. calls 'disavowal'.

Hugh looked in the phone book for me, and made a couple of calls, but could not find a trace of Derham.

He must have been very old by then, if still alive. It was almost certainly too late to talk to him. But still, but still — I let it go.

Hugh defended the integrity of his profession; why wouldn't he? ECT, for instance: many of Brian's friends and relations believed it scrambled his mind, but Hugh said it had been a widely used and well-respected treatment with significant evidence of benefits, particularly for depression.

Although, he added, it was perhaps less well proven in dealing with obsessional thoughts.

But what of the clamour of competing diagnoses? Could he adjudicate between them? Here, he cut through with a surgeon's sureness that I admired: 'He was obviously an obsessional personality. I think the stuff about pseudo-neurotic schizophrenia was rubbish.' Did you hear that, Zeck?

Obsessional thoughts, for example, 'I'm going to stab my baby with a knife,' intense and returning often, may become confused with delusions. Obsessive thoughts may be so powerful that they are experienced as coming from outside. But an obsessive knows that they are only thoughts, whereas a schizophrenic has no insight. Thus Brian, mowing his front lawn, knew he was imagining the voices in his head; knew he was quite alone and that they weren't real.

He may have had obsessive compulsive, or anankastic, disorder, continued Hugh. Obsessive compulsive: 'It's the same mechanism as children who walk on the footpath and don't step on cracks for fear of the bears — "I have to do this, otherwise something bad will happen." They recognise it's crazy, but they can't stop themselves doing it.'

With anxiety disorders, says Hugh, the more you resist, the better. The more you resist the temptations of the maze, the solving of the riddle, the more, in fact, you ignore the riddle.

There is one other thing that I need to ask Hugh before I leave the Swan River view. The first reference from 1945, 'some contact'? What does he make of this?

'Looks like he caught non-specific urethritis,' he says, 'Would have been caught most likely from a woman.' The prostitute in Little Lonsdale Street is suspect number one.

MEANWHILE, on 10 October 1963, Zeck continued. He and Brian had discussed leucotomy 'and its implications':

> He is agreeable to having it. I do not know what Dr Derham feels about the extent of operative interference but my personal opinion, bearing in mind that this is a severe (and becoming chronic) state, and that the man has good reserves of intelligence and drive, would be that a standard Freeman and Watts operation with a moderately posterior cut be carried out.

Zeck conceded that the operation could not proceed before Derham's return from holidays but, in the interim, sent Brian to see the surgeon who would perform the operation to obtain his agreement in principle to proceed. The surgeon commented, after discussing the situation with Brian, who appeared to him to be in a state of severe depression and confusion, that he 'was agreeable to undertake Freeman and Watts'.

Freeman and Watts: they could be an old legal firm. But a brief foray on the internet sets the mind spinning. Freeman and Watts pioneered lobotomy procedures in the United States in the 1930s and '40s.

I had thought a lobotomy would have been an operation of some precision, involving opening up the skull to snip some delicate incisions in the brain. It turns out that what they did in their 'standard operation' was to drill a hole in each side of the front of the head, insert a 'cutting instrument' in each hole, and 'sweep it in an arc' back and forth through the brain. What they cut, in any given case, was decidedly arbitrary.

They famously tried this out on Rosemary Kennedy, JFK's younger sister, in 1941. A passage from *The Sins of the Father*, a book on the Kennedy clan, describes the scene, beginning with a quote from Dr Watts:

'We went through the top of the head, I think she was awake. She had a mild tranquilizer. I made a surgical incision in the brain through the skull. It was near the front. It was on both sides. We just made a small incision, no more than an inch.' The instrument Dr. Watts used looked like a butter knife. He swung it up and down to cut brain tissue. 'We put an instrument inside,' he said. As Dr. Watts cut, Dr. Freeman put questions to Rosemary. For example, he asked her to recite the Lord's Prayer or sing 'God Bless America' or count backwards … 'We made an estimate on how far to cut based on how she responded.' … When she began to become incoherent, they stopped.

Formerly more or less intellectually disabled and prone to mood swings, the operation left Rosemary Kennedy completely incapacitated. She was hidden away until her death in 2005.

But the story gets stranger. It seems Dr Freeman thought the 'standard procedure' too costly and time-consuming to administer on a large scale in asylums, where he believed it was needed, and he became enthused about a new form of lobotomy wherein he literally hammered a metal spike, like an icepick, through the top of the eye socket and into the brain of the conscious patient. He went on to perform thousands of these 'icepick' lobotomies, at one time doing 225 in 12 days.

In the two weeks between 10 and 25 October 1963, before Derham returned and spoke with Brian, there was a fateful shift. This was the time that Wendy, making her way to the toilet long after her bedtime, accidentally overheard Brian, Joan, and Doris discussing the proposed operation in the lamplight of the Scarborough lounge room. This was the time that she worried he would be bald because they would shave his head; the time she read in the newspaper on the car seat that the president of America had been shot; the time Brian and Joan seriously contemplated the implications of leucotomy.

To sever some of the connections in your brain? The doctors could not say exactly what would happen, each time, which connections, how many. Your intelligence would not be affected, or so they hoped. But your personality: that would change. It's not clear how, exactly; but, after all, the whole point of the operation *was* to change your personality. Would you still be recognisably you? Would you still be there, if Joan looked into your eyes? Would you be — *a vegetable*?

No guarantees could be given. What kind of life would lie ahead, stretching out into the future? *If there is to be a game of Russian roulette*, thought Brian, *shouldn't it be I who pulls the trigger?*

Joan hoped against hope that leucotomy could be avoided. Perhaps if they moved away from Bridgetown? If Brian could be transferred to Perth, where he wouldn't have these long car trips alone. Or if the department could deploy another officer to accompany him as an assistant? Surely the worst could be avoided, her love would be enough. And how, if I might add, could he not be seduced by the eyes of that little baby?

It is not clear what Brian thought — whether he held out hope, or whether he was merely comforted by the knowledge that he was gathering the strength to kill himself, if and when he felt he must.

He rang Eric, who was teaching in Kalgoorlie, to ask his opinion. Eric told him that a lobotomy was a 'bloody ridiculous idea, you might as well die if you are going to do that. You would be just a zombie — if you do that, you don't worry about anything, because you can't'. No one was wildly in favour of the prospect.

By 25 October, Brian was expressing doubts about proceeding with the operation. But Derham was more concerned than ever with the risk facing him:

> I do advise prefrontal leucotomy as the surest means of preventing effective suicide. Earlier I have relied on his indecision to stay his hand but after four tentative attempts over a period of years this calculated risk becomes less justifiable … The undercurrent of distorted beliefs — regarding himself as a liar and a cheat for marrying, being sexually inadequate, and being dishonest in not having the courage to kill himself as he believes numerous other people have suggested by implication — these persist essentially unchanged.

Derham, I surmise, was worn out by Brian's case. He no longer hoped for a cure, and was ready to play any card that would merely keep this man alive.

But am I being unfair? After all, Derham imagined it was more than likely that Brian could continue with his work. In the best prospect, he would be substantially unaffected, with only the toxic sheep tracks severed. What if the surgeon could indeed cut out all the bad thoughts, leaving only the good behind? He would still feel love for his wife and children. It could be a miracle — and if the alternative is suicide? A decision was deferred another week.

On 1 November, Derham found Brian much improved. There was, Derham said, 'more evidence of insight than I have observed for a very long time in this man. He views his former self-destructive ideas as ridiculous and out of proportion, relating these to a building of inner tension through suppressing ideas of inadequate virility.'

Derham, for perhaps the first time, quoted Brian directly to indicate his levity: 'It is pretty silly if you think you've got to go and kill yourself to prove you're a man!'

Brian was enjoying an active exercise program at the hospital. He wanted to defer the leucotomy operation; both he and Joan agreed it would be desirable in the event of a recurrence. Given that he was feeling so well, it seemed hardly necessary to go ahead with it in the short term.

Derham now was inclined to agree, as was Zeck when he saw Brian a few weeks later. Zeck mused aloud about experimenting with some LSD abreaction therapy in an endeavour to rationalise Brian's thinking, to reduce the emphasis he placed on past 'traumatic' events. He never got a chance to try out this latest idea.

Brian was discharged from Hollywood on 5 November. Once again, he commenced work in Perth for a few days, then took the family back to Bridgetown. John and Wendy reunited with their school friends before the Christmas holidays.

On 19 December, Brian saw Derham one last time. Derham's notes are brief: 'Feeling well generally, apart from a persistent "cold". Has been active, busy and no mention is made of his symptoms today. He is having Largactil 25 mg. mane, 50 mg. nocte. Review in February, '64 recommended, provided he remains well meanwhile.'

Brian's very first recorded symptom, on 24 July 1945, at Flinders Naval Hospital, was a *common cold*. Now, at the end, it seems ironic somehow, after all he's been through, that it is a simple cold that remains persistent.

If I turn the page in the medical records, I find, without warning, a 'Report of Post-Mortem Examination'. Between one page and the next, he dies.

Chapter Fourteen

On the morning of 28 January 1964, Brian left home in the Falcon for a routine field trip to Kulikup, some few kilometres from Bridgetown. This was a day or two after Jim Frith saw him striding across the main street, 'bright and breezy'.

There was nothing untoward that morning. He said goodbye to Joan and the kids, as usual. He was planning to stay overnight at the Hardistys' farm and return later the next day.

Stan Hardisty, Brian's boss in the Agriculture Department office at Bridgetown, owned a property with his brother Charles in Kulikup that a man called Phil Lundy managed for them.

Stan and Brian both drove out to Kulikup that morning to take a look at the pastures and the condition of the sheep. At lunchtime, they went into the farmhouse with Phil to eat. For a time, they sat together in the lounge room smoking.

Why they wanted to sit in the lounge room at lunchtime instead of staying at the kitchen table is not clear. I have never been to, nor seen, this house. I can only imagine other farmhouse lounge rooms, other kitchens, where it would have made more sense for them to remain in the kitchen, near the back door and their dirty boots.

Because, you see, the way the story goes, it might have been different if they had never used the lounge room. The only gun on the farm was a .22 owned by Charles Hardisty, and this Phil had left standing that day in a corner of the lounge room, near where Brian happened to be sitting.

After lunch, both Stan and Brian left the Hardisty property. Phil later told the police that Brian displayed 'a normal and bright frame of mind'. Stan headed back to Bridgetown, and Brian continued on to Qualeup for an appointment with another farmer, John Cavanagh.

Brian and John passed the afternoon harvesting some experimental wheat plots that John had grown under Brian's direction. It was satisfying work, and Brian, according to John, 'appeared to be in the best of spirits'.

They didn't knock off until seven in the evening. Being the height of summer, the sun lingered in the sky at that hour of the day. John asked Brian if he had to drive all the way back to Bridgetown that night, but Brian said that he was staying over in the vicinity. John thought this meant that he would be going to Jack Stewart's place near Kojonup, as he sometimes did.

He last saw Brian 'standing beside his car which was parked on the Qualeup North Road adjoining the paddock in which the plots were situated'. A policeman duly noted down this detail.

What is not clear is whether Brian had arranged with Stan to stay the night at his farm, and if that is the reason he returned there from Cavanaghs, or if he already had in mind the gun.

Phil Lundy, as it happened, was driving up to Perth that evening. He left the farm at around 6.30 p.m. Sometime after that, Brian arrived back.

It seems probable Phil would have mentioned at lunchtime that he would be away that night.

The house, like any farmhouse in the district, was always left unlocked, and Brian would have been welcome to doss down in the spare room anytime he liked.

Usually, Phil would have locked the gun away in a cupboard, but on this occasion he forgot, so it was still propped up in the corner of the lounge room when Brian looked in. It wasn't loaded, but a box of ammunition lay on the bookcase.

I believe that when Brian saw the gun at lunchtime, leaning against the wall, the idea of suicide would have crossed his mind. Beyond shooting rabbits or kangaroos, Brian would have thought about himself, since the idea of self-destruction had been such a refrain in his head for years now. It might, at that time, have been nothing more than an idle thought in passing, even one he regarded with a healthy detachment as he contemplated the pleasant busy-work of the afternoon mini-harvest ahead.

Now, in the evening, he was alone in the quiet house, as alone as he had ever been. There was not even a telephone line installed. That gun of Hardisty's was still there. He'd fired guns before, of course, as a kid on his Uncle Jack's farm down at Wagin, and in the navy on the firing range. He'd had firearms training. He knew how to load a .22; there wasn't much to it. He knew how to pull the trigger.

This, in an instant, was the perfect opportunity. The gun was asking to be used. Now there could be no more excuses. This was his chance to prove himself, to do as *everyone had suggested*, in a thousand jokes and jibes, across all those years. And even if that was crazy, there was still his father shrugging his shoulders, turning away in disgust. *I will be setting everybody free,* he thought. *I am the dead weight pulling the boat under, only if I cut myself adrift can the rest survive.*

Who knows how long he lingered with the gun that night, whether he paced, whether he found it difficult to decide. I imagine that, once he had convinced himself of the logic of his actions, he was able to muster all his self-discipline and courage to keep himself from wavering.

In his own mind, this was the one heroic moment of a lifetime. Even as he lay down on the bed and took the loaded gun in his hands and shed tears for his wife and children, for his mother, for his brothers, for, maybe most of all, his father, he truly believed this was the best answer to the problem, the problem that could not be separated from his own existence. This was a better solution than leucotomy ... *You've been talking about it often enough, why don't you just go ahead and do it then?*

⁂

Once, during a summer holiday at Emu Point, near Albany, it may have been only weeks before he died, Brian took his old friend Pell Mann out on a dinghy with a little putt-putt outboard motor.

On one side of the point lay Oyster Harbour. Here, you could walk out on the mud and collect cockles, the water was calm and sheltered. On the other side of the point, which is in fact an isthmus, the water opens out into the great King George Sound. Far away are the islands of Michaelmas and Breaksea, and the granite promontories of the south, where the whalers docked.

Brian was at the tiller that day, and shouted to Pell recklessly, over the sound of the engine, the wind, and the ocean: 'Let's go out around the heads!' He wanted to travel beyond to where the big waves were. He said that Matthew Flinders had been all the way around Australia in a tiny vessel not much bigger. His 'bloody' Uncle Ben had been all the way across the Atlantic and round the world in an amphibious jeep, for Christ's sake. 'Come on, Pell, let's do it!'

'You're mad,' joked Pell. 'You're off your rocker, Baldy.'

'Yep, you're right there, I'm off my rocker. I'm going to bloody top myself, Pell. I'm gonna put cold steel in my mouth, Pell, cold steel in my mouth. You just watch me.' Which by this time was no longer funny.

'Come on, Brian, turn around, can you take me back, please? I don't want to go across the bloody bay and out into the ocean.' And Pell thought, *Why would he say that? That macho talk. Cold steel in my mouth.*

Some of the people whom I talked to who had known Brian well said that, while not endorsing or advocating what he did, in a way they believed that he was right — it was the best way out for all concerned.

It is confusing. Fogs descend into the valleys. Nothing has a clear shape in the mist. The sheep on the hillsides huddle together to keep warm under bare trees planted from seeds brought across the world to make this strange place seem more like home. I think of Walter Benjamin, Sylvia Plath. But am I forgetting? This is summer, the time of magpies, dry leaves hanging low among the gum trees, the river curling to a halt, brackish.

Bert Read knew a bloke called Jack who committed suicide; he used to own the other half of Bert's farm. This Jack was an ex-serviceman told to 'go out and get some fresh air', who couldn't make a go of it as a farmer. He was bad-tempered, moody (unlike Brian). And Pell Mann knew an advisor in the dairy division at the Agriculture Department, a delicate type at loggerheads with his boss — his name was Bob. Bob threw himself off the top balcony of the Royal Perth Hospital, but they said it couldn't be proved. He might have fallen. Pell laughed wryly, telling me that. Graeme Stewart, Joan's brother, said that in his district 'there's a lot more of it around than was ever admitted to'. He remembered Kevin O'Halloran, for one: he'd won a gold medal at the '56 Olympics, never seemed to be anything visibly wrong with him, but still …

❧

On the evening of the day of 29 January 1964, when Brian didn't come home to Bridgetown as expected, and after Joan had played the records on the turntable to make it seem as if nothing was yet the matter, she said to John and Wendy, 'We are all going to get into the big bed.' This, so far as I can tell, is how they slept that night. And I? Where was I? In the cot nearby? Or in the big bed, too, lying sideways like babies do, and kicking my tiny feet into their ribs?

In the morning, with still no sign of Brian, Joan waited, telling herself not to get alarmed, that there would be an explanation. Preparations continued for their holiday in Busselton; they were all packed up and due to leave that very day for a cottage rented by the beach, where Eric and Alison would join them.

It wasn't till two o'clock in the afternoon that she called Stan Hardisty. He said he hadn't heard from Brian since two days prior, but would drive out to his farm to check.

She knew already he was gone. But still, but still — he might be lying innocently ill or injured somewhere. There might be angels tending him, sucking out snake venom from the long grass. He might be fighting off a bushfire so well that the smoke wasn't even rising into the sky and the neighbours weren't alarmed. He might be so preoccupied, with his nose to the soil, listening to the subterranean clover grow, that he had forgotten all about the time and thought the stars were fireflies, and the darkness was a blanket the angels brought to keep away the chill. *One day he went to sleep and he never woke up.* How can you explain death to a small child?

Stan arrived at the farm and saw Brian's car parked outside

the house. He wished he hadn't seen it there. He wished Brian had turned up in Bridgetown by another road in his own absence, and had his feet up in the office, laughing at all the fuss.

Stan went into the back room and saw Brian on the bed, lying with the gun on top of him. And he saw the blood behind his head. He didn't need to touch him. He didn't need to take his pulse. 'Take my pulse,' Brian used to say to Eric in the pub. He wanted to take his own pulse all the time. Why? To see if he had started to die already — if his life was ebbing away, if his heart was slowing to a stop? Everyone told him not to be so *bloody ridiculous*. His brain was the problem. But now he had made a cut in it, and everything was quiet.

Stan backed out of the room and ran to the car. He drove across to the nearest phone, at Charlesworth's place. Hugh Charlesworth, who knew Brian, as did all the farmers more or less, was the first person he told. At 5.30 p.m.

Stan called Joan. She called her parents in Kojonup. That was the one thing she was able to do. Now I think about it, it may have been at this time that she said to the children, *We are all going to get into the big bed*. But this cannot be true because, when Jack and Barbara arrived 90 minutes later in their Jaguar, which I see sweeping around the corners with its majestic lines, its wood interior, its leather, its little wooden tables that folded out in the back seat, John and Wendy were playing in the front yard on their oversized tricycles, and they knew nothing yet; so Joan had not told them, and had held herself together as if in a trance.

Jack and Barbara got out of their car and said to John and Wendy, 'Please go around the back, we need to talk to your mum.' And some time later, after they had done what they were told for what seemed like ages, they came into the house through the back door and found Joan crying and sobbing, and she said to them, 'He's dead.' It was as if Jack and Barbara had brought the news.

'I remember a commotion, a hubbub, people standing around in the hall,' says Wendy. John says Mum was incredibly distressed; for us, he says, it was the end of the world as we knew it.

Someone — Jack Stewart? the police? — had phoned Doris in Scarborough. Noel took the call. He thought: there must have been a mistake. It was someone else they were talking about.

When he told Doris, 'she was all broken up'. So Noel said, 'hang on a minute' and went two doors down to Doug Hatch's place to bring Doug back with a bottle of brandy. 'We didn't have any grog in the house; we wouldn't have got through that evening without Doug Hatch being there for about three hours,' said Noel. It was up to Noel to make the phone calls to the family. He called Eric in Bunbury, but Eric was driving back from an Army Reserve camp, and it was Alison who answered and had to wait the several hours wondering how she would tell Eric when he arrived.

There was no way Joan was going to stay at the house in Bridgetown. The next day, the whole family would go back to Jack and Barbara's farm at Kojonup, where Joan had grown up. It was too late to travel that night, too dangerous in the dark. So it may have been at this time, finally, that Joan said to the children, *We are all going to get into the big bed.*

At some point in the evening, Eric and Alison arrived. The

children listened to the commotion and fell asleep. And the baby looked at the red eyes of its mother.

Joan wondered if the local priest would call to offer his support. She and Brian were at least Christmas and Easter church-goers. And Brian talked to the priest up at the Country Club quite often; this, she found out later.

The priest's name was Fred. Fred was partial to a drink or two at the club, or elsewhere. He liked to talk, at the bar and at the pulpit. Joan finally took it upon herself to speak to him. But Fred was cold. He didn't offer to organise a funeral for Brian at the church — suicides, he said, couldn't be buried in consecrated ground because the act of self-murder was a sin against God.

Jim Frith told me this was something else Brian mentioned that day in the ute parked at the top of the hill. 'Fred reckons it's the devil in me,' said Brian. In the days after Brian died, Jim rang Fred to see if he could find out the details of what had happened, but the priest seemed distant. He didn't want to carry on a conversation. Fred simply said to Jim down the thinness of the line, 'It's sad to lose our friends, isn't it?'

THE FAMILY LEFT the green weatherboard house in the morning and never went back.

For a week or two, they wrapped themselves up in the cool familiarity of Rocky Glen, and the children could observe the devastation that had taken hold of their mother.

Above anything, they didn't want to make it worse. After all, they had grown up knowing that good children must try never to upset the adults. If ever there was a time to show their goodness, it was now. They asked no questions. They waited and listened at the margins to the whispers. Wendy heard talk about plans for the funeral. She heard they were going to birth, or going to Perth. She couldn't tell which it was; she wanted to ask, but was too scared. What were they saying? Was it birth or Perth? What did any of it mean? It was like a fog, she says. She listened, wishing her little ears could bore into the long silences.

There was not much discussion at Barbara and Jack's. Very hush-hush. The devastation: after ten years of holding her breath amid the happy times, Joan simply fell and fell. The first sickening weightlessness of grief. Wendy, who was not yet seven, occupied herself tracing patterns on the blue-tiled windowsills.

This is not a time I ask Joan about in detail. Even now, the worst thing would be to upset her. We have already lost one parent without rhyme or reason. We must do everything to make sure the other one survives.

Both John and Wendy developed theories about what may have killed Brian. They discussed them not even with each other; they held them in deep compartments in their minds. Over time, Wendy made conjectures around cancer. There was the smoking, after all. And had she not seen him spitting phlegm? She knew it was something to do with the head, having tried the experiments in the toilet with the matchbox that time at Gran's house, so brain cancer seemed possible. A brain tumour, it was called. The weird thing: what did it have to with the war? Why were she and John members of Legacy, which was for kids whose dads had died in wars?

Why, after they'd moved to Perth, did they have to go to

Legacy gym club in the city every Saturday morning?

John knew it had to be something that caused sudden death. After all, his father had not been sick in hospital for weeks beforehand, or coughing for months on end, or limping. He had been as tall as ever the last time he saw him.

John considered that it might have been a snake. He had read in a *Boy's Own Annual* about an explorer in India who woke up with a cobra in his sleeping bag. Brian had once told a story about a family that had run over a snake but not killed it. The snake became caught up, somehow, underneath the car, and they found it under the bonnet. Whether dead or alive is no longer clear, but John says that, after Brian died, 'there were months if not years I would check the bed for snakes'.

Whatever happened to Brian could happen to any of us. There seemed to be a weakness in the family that could strike at any time, *causing sudden death*. John developed anxieties around growing pains.

Would we all have been better off to have more information? Much later, when the truth came out, we thought his madness, too, might be congenital. Or his sadness, if that was what it was.

In the days and weeks after Brian died, Jack Stewart took control, assuming the role of protector for his daughter. He arranged the private funeral at Karrakatta Cemetery in Perth.

Few were invited: family, plus some but not all of Brian's close friends. Under the circumstances, it seemed the less fuss the better. Eric and Andrew went, of course, but not Noel, for some reason. It appears he was left at Scarborough to look after

Doris, with Alison. Men's business, this was. Did Noel not make the grade?

Joan's brother Graeme was among the mourners; in the procession, he travelled in the car with Jack and Joan's brother-in-law, Pell.

Joan herself remained behind at Rocky Glen with her mother and the children, waiting, making an effort to drink tea with civilised decorum, the house closed up against the heat.

BIRTH OR PERTH — which was it? A return to Bridgetown was out of the question. There was nothing left there now. They wouldn't say goodbye to their friends; they would simply vanish like genies into thin air. They couldn't stay forever at Rocky Glen. Joan must have a chance to start again. Perth was the obvious answer: Doris could help out with the children, Joan find herself a job. Henry Schapper was already talking of projects she could work on for him at the university.

Within a fortnight, Jack had found a house in the same street as an old family friend. He took Joan up to look at it, and put a deposit down the same day.

John and Wendy were enrolled at a nearby primary school before the school year began in early February. Their old life was over, and a completely new and different one begun.

Once, not long later, Joan showed John a clipping from an agriculture journal that contained a eulogy to Brian. 'I don't want you to forget your dad,' she said. 'This is what they wrote about him.'

But, from the moment they arrived in Perth, she took the

entire responsibility for grieving upon herself. Brian's death was discussed neither with the children nor in the family at large. This wasn't to be a burden anybody else would carry for her. And nobody else wanted to be the one to speak first.

John was concerned that the kids at his new primary school would ask questions. Over time, he found it sufficed to simply say, 'He died.' The other children were not brave enough to ask for further details, so he didn't need to worry about how to make them up.

Messages are delivered in silences.

☙

At 15, John came across Brian's death certificate in the hallway bureau. The certificate contained the words 'self-inflicted gunshot wound'. Spelt out clearly: *self-inflicted*. But still, but still … John considered the ways in which it could have been an accident. At least he knew now that it wasn't a heart attack. And, as he told himself, he'd put to bed years ago the childish snake-bite theory.

How do you shoot yourself? Because surely not deliberately? That would imply mental illness, and *that* would mean any of us could be mentally ill. He put the certificate back into the bureau and didn't look at it again. He told no one. After all, he shouldn't have been snooping there in the first place. Suicide, the idea, he put in a box and swallowed.

When is a good time to begin talking about these things?

Joan made a new life as a single mother. Her family, and the Carlins, wrapped themselves around her. Her children were happy, performed well at school. She made a valued contribution to the university's new Farm Management Service Laboratory, which encouraged farmers to count everything they could and send in the data to be typed onto punch cards for a computer the size of a small apartment.

In the holidays, the family went on camping trips, or down to Rocky Glen.

One summer, we even flew all the way to New Zealand in a Boeing 727 to see the boiling mud pools and the glaciers, the black swans at the Perth Airport, the rain in Sydney going, the water-wall in Melbourne coming back.

Wendy, at university, still lived at home, although all her friends had set up share-houses. She felt she could not abandon Joan to be alone with the baby (even though he was now 13 or more). John had moved out long ago, finished university, and gone backpacking to Spain. Wendy was confused as to what she should do.

The year she turned 20, she moved out temporarily to stay with friends. One night, she came home for dinner. She was drying the dishes, while Joan washed — an action they had shared many times before.

Suddenly, tea towel in hand, as they were both busy by the sink, Wendy asked: 'How *did* Dad die?'

A brain tumour, Joan would say. Even then, Wendy was quite sure of it. Instead, Joan said to the soapy water, 'He committed suicide.' Just like that, no more. All other words were sucked out of the narrow kitchen, the air inside not strong enough to bear them.

Wendy fled, but politely, because it was a race to see who could upset the other least.

The friends whom she stayed with were university teachers, older than she. After a day or so of quiet panic and hyperventilation, she told them everything she knew and didn't know, and they looked after her.

Frank, the man she was staying with, took her to the cemetery to find Brian's plaque. They arranged for her to see Hugh Cook, and from this came the family meeting at Hugh's clinic, where your narrator was told the news.

❧

I once imagined an ending. A scene on a beach where the family came together and lit a huge funeral pyre. There may have been candles, too. Now, as I think of it again, it seems to be a tropical beach. The ritual takes on an Asian flavour: Hindu perhaps. Colourful tents, elephants. There is a momentous release of energy in the fire. We cast more and more timbers on the flames: driftwood washed ashore, coconut shells, pinecones from Cottesloe Beach. It reminds me of one time when we camped out in the red desert sands of Western Australia and burnt an entire dead tree for the evening campfire. A whiff of pyromania runs in the family.

Acknowledgements

This book began life as part of a PhD project at the University of Melbourne. There, Kevin Brophy's astute questions and calm, sharp eye helped me immeasurably, as I took my first steps into the unknown. Scott McQuire, Sari Smith, Christine Owen, and Brian Castro, among many others, provided invaluable early comments.

Without the support of my family, the book would not have been possible. My uncle Eric and aunt Alison Carlin always welcomed me when I visited Perth, and it was they, more than anyone, who revealed the family's stories, opened up a treasure-box of images and documents, suggested and helped locate people whom I could interview, and drove me across the city and beyond, to show me various places that were important in my father's life. My other Carlin uncles, Andrew and Noel, and my mother's brother Graeme and sister Margaret, generously gave me their time and hospitality, and my cousin Michael offered very helpful feedback on work-in-progress. My siblings John and Wendy made crucial contributions, both in being interviewed and in making detailed comments on the first draft of the manuscript.

Perhaps most important was the participation and 'blessing' of my mother, Joan, for whom the memories I was excavating were the most intimate and painful. My mother is quite an extraordinary person, as all who know her will agree, and she has shown a remarkable strength and openness in encouraging me to pursue the story however I saw fit.

Many of my father's former friends, colleagues, and naval shipmates also assisted by sharing their stories and photographs, and by chasing down further contacts for me. I thank them all.

Jeff Sparrow and Rjurik Davidson at *Overland* provided a wonderful avenue for a version of the first chapter to be published. Thanks to all the friends I have drawn upon for help in all sorts of ways, and especially, for the writerly advice, to Melissa Reeves, Catherine McKinnon, Wayne Macauley, and Patricia Cornelius. Thanks, too, to my colleagues at the RMIT School of Media and Communication, for their encouragement and support.

My publisher, Henry Rosenbloom, and editor, Nicola Redhouse, and all their colleagues, have been an absolute pleasure to work with, ever since our first emails. Their commitment to the book has been unstinting, and Nicola has brought joy, passion, and rigour, in equal parts, to the editorial process.

My children, Esther and Louis, have gracefully accepted the

writing of this book, stretching across several years of their young lives, inspired me with their wit and kindness, and granted me space to write in the mornings on many beach holidays.

Finally, my partner, Linda Mickleborough, to whom the book is dedicated, inspired me to even contemplate the project in the first place: her unwavering love and commitment, ideas, good humour, forbearance, and optimism, have been the essential sweet ingredients in enabling its completion.